Praise for S

"An important book for anyone who wants to succeed in life! It outlines powerful strategies that would help you and your business go further while bringing you greater happiness and success in all areas of your life."

Barbara A. Glanz, Author
CARE Packages for the Workplace,
Handle with CARE, and Balancing Acts

"Reading Stop Singing the Blues doesn't just give you a philosophy of how to live a better life, it gives you a friend for life--a friend who shares her life journey with you, holding your hand in your journey and making every step of the way easier, more interesting and exciting. But most of all, she gives you the heart to have a better life, in fact the best life possible. Thank you Cynthia, You're a treasure and so is your book!"

Joycebelle
Founder www.GoodStoryaDay.com
Enriching the World: one story, one child, one day at a time!

"WOW! I have just finished reading *Stop Singing the Blues*, and I was blown away. I was instantly drawn into the first chapter by compelling real life examples Dr. Barnett shares about how she and other women have triumphed over great odds to move to the pinnacle of success. I have read hundreds of personal and professional development books, but this one is different. *Stop Singing the Blues* is truly magical! Once you start reading *Stop Singing the Blues*, you won't want to put it down. It is truly a masterpiece!"

Bea Fields
President
Five Star Leader Coaching and Training
www.FiveStarLeader.com

"If you are serious about empowerment, the concepts in this book will blow you away."

Dave Brown
Author of *Protect Your Home*

"I've had the privilege of knowing Cynthia for many years and have watched her live her dreams. She is the embodiment of the strategies she writes about. This book is the result of her working the principles she practices daily. If you want to realize your deepest desires, too, learn how by reading *Stop Singing the Blues*."

Jane Pollak
Author of *Soul Proprietor: 101 Lessons from
a Lifestyle Entrepreneur*
and *Decorating Eggs: Exquisite Designs with Wax & Dye*

"Doctor Cynthia is a woman who walks her talk. Her personal story is inspiring and this book will help anyone who is serious about their dreams."

Marcia Wieder
America's Dream Coach
Author, *Making Your Dreams Come True*

"This book is outstanding! It shows you how to use simple strategies to build your inner resilience so that you can have all the success you deserve."

Glenna Salsbury
CSP, CPAE Speaker Hall of Fame
Past President of National Speakers Association

"Dr. Cynthia's writing style is SO easy to read and using real-life people and their stories to make her points is incredibly easy to learn from. Her thought-provoking questions and easy to use exercises are very helpful for personalizing the material for the reader. I think everyone knows someone who has broken through some difficult barriers but don't get the social chance to find out. Here Dr. Cynthia opens a window into those people's souls and gracefully shares it with her readers.

Abby Marks-Beale
Author of *10 Days to Faster Reading*

"Here is the toolkit for anyone who wants to succeed in life. These compelling stories and powerful strategies will help you and your business go further and set you on a path toward greater happiness and success in all areas of your life."

Helen Goodman
Business Coach, and formerly Senior Vice President,
Human Resources, The Hartford Financial Services Group, Inc.

"You hold within your hands a masterpiece of wisdom, wit and insight. What a pleasure to be asked to write a Foreword for such a book. You, the reader, will quickly see that the information in this book has not been developed from the 'ivory tower' but in the real world. You will see that if you put into practice even a fraction of the strategies that are very clearly and eloquently developed, you would sing a new song in your life."

Gerry Robert
Best-selling author of *The Millionaire Mindset*

"This book will inspire you to be the best that you can be. It will give you the confidence to overcome challenges so that you can accomplish anything you want."

Robert G. Allen
Best-selling author of *The One Minute Millionaire and Nothing Down*

"This is a wonderful book. Reading this book is a transforming experience. The coaching principles are as sound as the Rock of Gibraltar and are explained with such clarity you will never forget them. As a teacher with an abundance of inspiration and creativity, relevant lessons on how to live an exciting, balanced life, Dr. Cynthia is unsurpassed."

Christian D. Warren
Author of *Running with the Rhinos; Transforming Yourself Into A Leader Others Will Gladly Run With*

"Brilliant! A formidable piece of writing guaranteed to get you out of that rut and rethink your life's priorities. Full of action plans to stop procrastination and set you on the track to a better life."

Rozieta Shaary
Best-selling author of *Happy Kids*

"This is a must read book for women everywhere. An invaluable book to the insights of becoming a stronger more balanced person who contributes to the betterment of the world."

Susan Harley
Author of *Gentle Hands*

"One of the most practical handbooks I have ever come across. I was especially impressed by Dr. Cynthia's insights into how to change the music of one's life."

Victor Kim
Co-author of *Shoot for the Moon*

"As a woman and as an entrepreneur I know a great book when I see one. *Stop Singing the Blues* is such a book. Life and business can be tough. What this book does is provide a step-by-step plan to live a better, more fulfilled and balanced life. It shows you how to turn things around. A hit!"

Jean Ann Dorrell
Author of *Protect Yourself*

For additional information, address your questions to:
publishing@e2ibooks.com

Published by e2i Books
1800 Pembrook Drive 3rd Floor
Orlando, FL 32810

The e2i Books name and logo are registered trademarks of e2i Books
Cover and book design by: e2i Books

Visit our website at: www.e2ibooks.com or email us at: publishing@e2ibooks.com

Printed in the United States of America
First edition e2i Books printing: May 2005

Library of Congress Cataloging-in-Publication Data
Barnett, Cynthia, 1943-
Stop singing the blues: 10 powerful strategies for hitting the high notes in your life / Cynthia Barnett.-- 1st ed.
        p. cm.
    ISBN 0-9763177-2-9 (pbk. : alk. paper)
 1. Life skills--Handbooks, manuals, etc. I. Title.
        HQ2037.B37 2005
        158.1--dc22   200500848
        10 9 8 7 6 5 4 3 2 1

Stop Singing the Blues

10 Powerful Strategies

for

Hitting the High Notes in Your Life

Dr. Cynthia Barnett

Dedication

I dedicate this book to the memory of my mother, Linda London, who had the courage and tenacity to actively achieve her dreams by coming to America and making a better life for herself and her four children. Also, to my life mate Harry, who has supported and encouraged me through this entire project. And to my three daughters Debbie, Malene, and Nneka, who have been the drive behind my passion to achieve my dreams.

Finally, I dedicate this book to you, the reader. This book is all about building a strong foundation so that you can have a meaningful, abundant, and successful life.

To My Readers

We've all been born with the potential for living a fulfilled, happy, and enjoyable life. Some of us have achieved extraordinary success in business and in life; some of us have watched others achieve it; some of us have wondered what happened to us.

If you're among those asking, "Where is success for me?" read on!

Stop Singing the Blues addresses the slumbering giant inside of you that feels stuck, dissatisfied, frustrated, and afraid. Its ten strategies aim to ignite the fire within you, to awaken you to the fulfillment, happiness, and joy you've been yearning for.

The simple but powerful tools in this book help you tap into an inner strength that builds your foundation for an extraordinary life. They're available to you right now—in fact, they're so readily available, they can be easily missed.

I'm hoping that reading the true stories in *Stop Singing the Blues* gives you assurance that you're not alone. Don't just read the words; digest their meaning over and over as you apply them to your life. As many have discovered, the strategies really work.

Please know that the "yes" deep inside of you is your God-given power to have a fulfilled, satisfying, and joyous life. You deserve it!

—Dr. Cynthia Barnett

Acknowledgments

While I knew there was a book inside me, I couldn't bring it out by myself. I needed the support and help of many people. I'm grateful for all those who helped me successfully complete this book. My deepest thanks goes to these wonderful people:

My writing mentor, Melaney Gabris, for her indispensable help in collaborating, editing, cheerleading, enthusiastically supporting, and believing in the message of this book. The experience rewarded us both because we share interests in improving the lives of women and making a difference.

Marcia Powell for her interviewing and editorial skills, and Barbara McNichol for her editing contribution on the final manuscript.

Gerry Robert for sharing my vision and enthusiasm for this book, and providing guidance and support for its production.

All the "unstoppable women" who freely shared their inner feelings and experiences to show others that they, too, can overcome obstacles.

Women in my retreats and workshops who constantly asked, "Do you have a book?" Their questions and encouragement planted the seed for the birth of this book.

—Dr. Cynthia Barnett

Table of Contents

Foreword

You hold within your hands a masterpiece of wisdom, wit and insight. What a pleasure to be asked to write a Foreword for such a book. You, the reader, will quickly see that the information in this book has not been developed from the "ivory tower" but in the real world. You will see very early on in this book that if you put into practice even a fraction of the strategies that are very clearly and eloquently developed, you would sing a new song in your life.

The other thing one will quickly notice by reading this great book is that the author knows what she is talking about and that the material is lived out in her life. I have such a high regard for Dr. Barnett. It's no wonder to me that she is in such demand as a speaker and as a coach to high achievers. She actually lives out the material in this book. She is living proof that one can Stop Singing the Blues.

If you want a book that is practical, sometimes funny, sometimes touching, sometimes moving, sometimes confrontational but always effective to help you live a more pleasant, more effective life, then this is the book for you. In one aspect it has nothing really to do with "music" but in another, it has everything to do with "music." That "music" is your life MUSIC. It's the harmony you feel on the inside. It's the melody of your dreams and aspiration. It'll make you dance with joy when you apply it to your life.

The reason I'm so proud of writing the Foreword for this wonderful book is that I know how many people it will help. I have read thousands of books, written several myself, and I know the power of a good book when I see one. This is one such book. Read it, highlighter in hand, and act on it.

Congratulations Dr. Barnett for giving the world one more reason to sing a little brighter, dance a little sweeter and enjoy the "music" of life a little deeper.

A powerful book by a powerful writer who knows how to reach down and touch your heart! I highly recommend it!"

—Gerry Robert
Best Selling author
The Millionaire Mindset

Introduction

Veronica ran up to me after one of my seminars. With tension and anxiety written all over her face, she begged for a few minutes of my time. Totally exhausted after an all-day seminar, I couldn't wait to get home to rest, so I handed her my card and asked her to call me. Her look of disappointment stopped me in my tracks. I agreed to give her a few minutes.

That was one of the best decisions of my life. You see, Veronica had operated a successful business for ten years but was feeling frustrated and down. Stuck and empty, her life wasn't going the way she planned. She knew there was something more but couldn't pinpoint it.

We talked for more than two hours as I went into more detail about the strategies I had just shared in my seminar. Her eyes lit up and she said, "This is just what I was looking for!" She committed to use some of the strategies on a daily basis.

Months later, she called to share her excitement about the changes in her life and how fulfilled she felt. Her quality of life was enhanced and her business became even more successful. I was so glad I had stayed to talk with her—because this discussion gave birth to this book!

BUILD A FOUNDATION

The strategies in this book are the same ones I shared with Veronica. They made such a difference in her life and I'm confident they'll also enhance yours. They're simple, but not easy. They can change your life, too, but aren't a "quick-fix." Yet I know in my heart these foundational strategies to overcome adversities will help you become even more successful and fulfilled.

Building a skyscraper doesn't start at street level. Builders have to construct a strong foundation so the structure can withstand the elements through the centuries. So it is with life. A strong foundation holds you up. *Stop Singing the Blues* shows you how to dig a deep foundation that will last a lifetime.

Specifically, each chapter shows you how to unearth your dormant strengths and rediscover the real *you*. You'll read stories about people, like you, who had been frustrated, depressed, or stuck, and you'll learn how they broke free from whatever held them back. Pay special attention to the key strategies at the end of each chapter; they will help you stay focused and take action.

This book will help you discover how to:
- Enjoy increased creativity and productivity.
- Arouse the sleeping greatness within you.
- Love and appreciate your own uniqueness.
- Banish fears and doubts in 30 minutes.
- Cultivate an attitude of gratitude.
- Inject excitement into your life.

Charge your soul with fire to live with joy and abundance.

Are you ready to cut the wires holding you back? Are you ready to eliminate thoughts that keep you down and actions that prevent you from living the life you want? If you are, come with me to hit the high notes of courage, confidence, and joy.

I guarantee that if you make a commitment to change and pursue these foundational strategies with diligence, you'll become more successful and productive. Most importantly, you'll experience more joy, fulfillment, and satisfaction.

"There are three ingredients in the good life: learning, earning, and yearning." —Christopher Morley

"The only way to live is to accept each minute as an unrepeatable miracle which is exactly what it is—a miracle and unrepeatable."
—Margaret Storm Mameson

MY BIG DREAM

Forty years ago, I arrived in the United States with no money, no career guidance, and no resources—but I had a *big dream:* to get the best education that this country had to offer. I had no idea how that was going to happen; however, I was willing to do whatever it took to achieve my *dream.* That meant to get through college, I had to work various jobs, including cleaning houses, filing documents for an insurance company, waiting tables in a convalescent home, even inserting the ink in ball-point pens in a pen factory.

Many obstacles stood in my way and I often felt overwhelmed, but I always saw the light at the end of that tunnel—the fulfillment of my dream. The obstacles I faced included divorcing after a 12-year marriage, gaining excessive weight, parenting as a single mother, suffering low self-esteem, and supporting three children on little money.

Through persistence, hard work, and constant focus on my personal development, I achieved my dream of earning the highest degree in my field and put all three of my daughters through college. My first daughter is an attorney, my second is a freelance surface design artist, and my third is a teacher.

I'm still fulfilling my destiny: to help women like you fulfill *your* dreams so that you, too, can experience a life of passion, peace, clarity, and happiness.

I'm confident that the experiences I outline in this book will prove to be valuable resources for you. These strategies worked for me and for those who've learned them through my coaching, workshops, retreats, and keynote speeches. I know they'll work for you, provided that you *take action* and apply them.

Chapter 1

Somewhere Over the Rainbow: Big Dreams

"You have got to have a dream if you want to make a dream come true." —Rodgers and Hammerstein

We all possess the power to dream. Many of us have chosen not to use the power as we've gotten older, but we all had big dreams when we were little. We had visions of becoming ballerinas, singers, dancers, teachers, mothers, doctors, lawyers, and maybe even the president of the United States. We played dress up and hung posters on our walls with our dream cars and mates.

What was your dream? How many times did you think to yourself, "When I grow up, I'm going to...." Maybe you were going to buy all the candy you wanted or get a particular car. Perhaps you had a certain house in mind with a swimming pool or a boat. Maybe you wanted to help others or simply care for ten cats and dogs. But something happened along the way and you gave up on your dreams. You just quit.

A small percentage of the population did go on to achieve big dreams. What's the difference between them and you? Were their dreams more important? No. More realistic? Probably not. Were they smarter people than you? Prettier? Luckier? No to all of these. But they had the burning desire to achieve their dreams, they acted in spite of their fears, and they tuned out the opinions of those who didn't encourage them.

If you've given up on your dreams, reread the previous

paragraph. Which reason applies to you? Did you have a burning desire to reach your dreams? Did you let your fears prevent you from taking action? Did you believe someone who told you it wouldn't work, or look around and see other people not reaching their dreams and just assume you shouldn't reach yours? Your honest answers to these questions hold the reason why you put your dreams on a shelf. If your dreams are on a shelf, they have no chance of coming true until you pull them off and place them in the line of your focus.

WHAT'S YOUR DREAM?

Don't fret if you can't remember what your dreams were. It's not unusual to be in the middle of adulthood and not be able to think of any dreams for yourself. Life got in the way. You got busy with the lives of others, probably because you had to. If you have trouble thinking of any dreams, you likely haven't been giving yourself enough attention. That's okay. Enjoy this chapter and get ready to enjoy your life more!

"Conditions are never just right. People who delay action until all factors are favorable do nothing."
–William Feather

You probably don't have everything you need to make your dreams come true. If you did, they already would have come true. Earlier, when I mentioned the differences between those who achieve their dreams and those who don't, I never said that they knew everything they needed to know. Don't think you have to know everything, or have all the resources, or know how you're going to make your dream come true. That will come later. Gerry Robert said something powerful in his instructions for writing out your Heart's Desires (see Chapter 2). He said, "Don't worry about whether you can afford it, if you know how to get it, or if you have other obstacles in the way. Just list what you want."

Half the fun will be the journey – watching everything come together. Remarkable things happen when you decide what you want. Opportunities will come that were probably there all along, but you don't notice them until they fit a dream you want to fulfill. When you're watching for the elements you need, life is an enjoyable experience.

WHOM DO YOU HANG OUT WITH?

Consider the five people you spend the most time with. Are they positive and encouraging, or negative and cynical? What are their lives like? Do they have the results that you want in your life? "Show me who you frequently spend time with and I will tell you who you are," reads a French proverb. Ask yourself if they are dream-makers or dream-breakers. If you have a burning desire to reach your dreams, you'll surround yourself with like-minded people. If you don't have a burning desire, you'll probably continue to keep the same company and get the same results you do now.

If you're thinking, "This doesn't affect me—this applies to other people," then you really need to pay attention. Your subconscious mind absorbs everything at face value—including the opinions of other people. Just as recovering alcoholics can't spend time with their drinking buddies or frequent bars if they expect to continue their sobriety, you can't afford to be around negativity if you're serious about reaching your dreams. There is a price.

"What great thing would you attempt if you knew you could not fail?" –Dr. Robert Schuller

Use this quote from Dr. Schuller to help you start identifying your dreams. Enjoy reading these stories and then take action with the suggestions listed at the end of this chapter.

My Dream Come True

Who would have believed that the petite, self-assured, successful woman who held the position of assistant principal in a high school was the same young girl who arrived in the United States 40 years before without money, resources, or guidance in how she'd achieve her big dream? Who could have imagined that this same young woman had to dig in the bottom of her purse searching for coins to take the train home to the Bronx where she lived with her mother, stepfather, and a two-year-old brother in a one-bedroom apartment? Or that she was the same young woman who cleaned houses, filed documents for an insurance company, waited tables in a convalescent home, and worked in a pen factory inserting the ink in ball-point pens to achieve her dreams?

As you know from the introduction, this is my story. Many obstacles stood in my way and I often felt overwhelmed, but I kept the vision alive. My *dream* was an obsession. I had a burning desire to earn the highest degree colleges had to offer in my field.

Success didn't come easy. I had to work every step of the way. This part of my story followed my divorce, which you'll read about in Chapter 5. I struggled to get into college. When I auditioned for music school, I was told that my skills weren't up to standard. Not ready to give up, I asked what I needed to do to gain admittance. They told me to hire a teacher and practice. I did and was accepted. While working on my doctorate degree, I had to retake the certification examination. I was not deterred by these failures. Instead, I used them as lessons to get to the next step.

I became a teacher. When a position for which I was highly qualified opened up in my school district, I was rejected and I filed a lawsuit – a story you'll read in the chapter on strengths (Chapter 6).

All of these experiences made me stronger and more confident. Now that I've "retired" from the school system, I've "refired" my life as an entrepreneur with a passion for helping other women turn their dreams into reality.

Mary's Ivy League Dream

Watching the Oprah TV show, I was touched by the story of Mary Shodiva who came to this country from Nigeria with a *big* dream to get the best education from an Ivy League school. Her heart was set on Columbia University. She knew that her grades had to be excellent and her class ranking high. She achieved both and was admitted into Columbia University. But she had no money to pay for her education and couldn't get financial aid because she wasn't a citizen, so she devised a gutsy plan to make her dream a reality.

She created a large sign that said, "Hello! I'm Mary. I am brilliant. Columbia University agrees. All I need is a loan. Name your interest rate." She went to Wall Street using the sign to tell the whole world her story. She was so desperate for help and the fulfillment of her dream that she was ready to achieve both by any means necessary.

Judith Aidoo, owner of an investment firm on Wall Street, saw the sign and was impressed. She spread the word to all her friends and other companies. In less than six weeks, they had collected over $40,000 from people all over the world to fund Mary's education at Columbia University. Currently a student at Columbia University, she can hardly believe her good fortune. What a lesson in never, never giving up and holding onto a *dream*.

Dr. Faith's Doctorate Dream

The room exploded with clapping and congratulations for Faith Sample. At her 15th high school reunion, she had stunned her classmates by being the one with a Ph.D.—an astounding accomplishment! Who would have thought that Faith, one of 13 children, would earn her doctorate from Cornell University? Not her guidance counselor, who was a big discouragement to her and provided no help with the college process; not her classmates who were skeptics and thought that one of their three black classmates was "dreaming" when she said she would become a doctor. But unlike them, she fully expected her dream to become a reality, so her accomplishment didn't surprise her. At the age of seven, she knew what she wanted. She wanted to teach and be a doctor.

Faith grew up in a middle-class neighborhood. Her father worked as a foreman at a nearby factory while her mother remained at home to take care of all 13 children. The eighth child, Faith was extremely shy and introverted. Her only friends and playmates were her younger brothers and sisters. She grew up thinking that her brother, who was five years older than she, was assigned to take care of her. He walked her to school, protected her, and was there for her in both positive and negative ways. Because she believed him to be her protector, Faith thought nothing of him fondling her, which started when she was six and continued until she was 14.

At the end of her senior year of high school, Faith was thankful for the day when her older sister, a Howard graduate, told her how to get into college. She wasn't close to her older sister, so she didn't share her intention of going to college until she was on the verge of graduating. She scrambled to get her application completed and recommendations in order. She was accepted into Howard University at the last minute with a major in education. She credits God for watching out for her.

Faith left home three weeks after her high school graduation, moved in with her sister in Washington, D.C., found several odd jobs, and started saving for her education. For four years, she studied at Howard full-time while working full-time. She didn't have time to think, only to work and complete her assignments. Her fear of failure propelled her to achieve. Finally, when she graduated, she was so exhausted that she took a year off before she entered graduate school.

Now that she had more time to think, memories of the molestation surfaced and Faith began to see a therapist. Coming close to having an emotional breakdown, her sessions with the therapist saved her life. Through intensive therapy, she was able to face her brother who was hoping that she didn't remember. The disclosure caused a great rift in the family as her father blamed her mother for not being aware of what was going on, and the other siblings alienated her. It has taken many years for the family to heal. Her brother continues to remain distant and aloof.

Faith credits getting her determination and drive from her father, who inspired her by his example. He overcame asthma by starting to run at age 40, taught himself Spanish, learned to do the renovations around the house including electrical work and plumbing, and encouraged his children to volunteer by cleaning up the neighborhood and helping others. His values filtered down to Faith, who became highly goal-oriented and focused.

After a year off from school, Faith applied and was accepted into Cornell University's Ph.D. program. This was the beginning of another grueling process. She also adopted a two-year-old, the child of a niece who couldn't take care of her daughter. On top of working on her Ph.D. and taking care of a toddler, she had to work. Her determination and focus on her dream kept her going.

Finally, Faith's last semester ended. She vividly remem-

bers the incredible relief she felt driving home after defend-
ing her dissertation. She recalls her shoulders dropping, the
stress going away, and the astounding feeling that she had
achieved her dream of becoming a teacher and a doctor.
Today, on the door of one of the offices in a prestigious Ivy
League School, Columbia University, is engraved the name
"Dr. Faith Sample."

"Everything is theoretically impossible, until it is
done. One could write a history of science in reverse
by assembling the solemn pronouncements of highest
authority about what could not be done and could
never happen." –Robert Heinlein

"The idea is to seek a vision that gives you purpose
in life and then to implement that vision. The vision by
itself is one half, one part, of a process. It implies the
necessity of living that vision, otherwise the vision will
sink back into itself." –Lewis P. Johnson

"If you take responsibility for yourself, you will
develop a hunger to accomplish your dreams."
–Les Brown

"The most pathetic person in the world is
someone who has sight but has no vision."
–Helen Keller

STUMBLING BLOCKS

Consider the following stumbling blocks. Are you tripping over any of them?

The Age Factor

Colonel Sanders started his successful KFC business when he was 65. Success doesn't depend on age, rather on the desire to dream, and the courage to realize the dream.

Lacking Vision

Vividly visualize your dream, taking it to sleep, thinking constantly about it, talking about it, planning it, adding all the spices. Your vision will take you a bit closer to the realization of your dreams.

Having No Idea

Entrepreneurship starts with a dream: a simple wish of a tiny restaurant, or a huge real-estate development business, or a modest training center for English education, or any other self-employed, money-earning idea.

Indefinite Deadline

The ability to dream is one of the fine qualities of the human race that other species don't possess. So dream on and assign a deadline: make it a giant dream, a tiny one, an old everlasting one, a newfound one, a hobby-related one, a change-of-life one, a religious one, a stupid one, a stroke-of-genius one, whatever. Just continue to dream on—then, go and do.

KEY STRATEGIES TO IGNITE AND LIVE YOUR DREAM

Write down your dreams. Make a list of everything you would like to have, no judgments or telling yourself that they are impossible. Just do it!

Break them down into baby steps. After all, a journey of a thousand miles begins with a single step. Identity the obstacles that keep you away from your dreams and overcome them by developing a personal action plan. Then take your first step—it will get you moving in the direction of your dreams.

Find people who will support you, people who love you and will be your cheerleaders. Let them know how much you appreciate them as they cheer you on to success.

Visualize each dream you have on a daily basis. Paint a vivid picture of your dream in your mind—see it, feel it. Let your imagination flow and watch the magic happen as your dream becomes reality.

Chapter 2

I Can Fly:
Believe in Yourself

"Believe in yourself! Have faith in your abilities!
Without a humble, but reasonable confidence in your
own powers, you cannot be successful or happy."
—Norman Vincent Peale

Belief is an important element to your success; in fact, it's critical. You could apply what you learned from the other chapters in this book, but if you disregard belief, your results will not be what you envisioned.

"If you think you can do a thing or think you can't
do a thing, you're right." —Henry Ford

Have you ever seen a talented person, perhaps a musician or an athlete, crack under pressure? When it came to performing for a major event, the person choked or got results that took him out of first place, yet he had the ability to do better. This happens when people don't have inner belief in themselves or their abilities. Without belief, people sabotage themselves.

You must believe you can have what you want and that you deserve it—that you're worthy. How else can you expect to get it? If you don't believe you deserve what you want, just change your belief. Easier said than done, right? I've got great news: When you start to believe you can have what you want and that you deserve it, you'll feel like a new person. With a fresh outlook, you'll be amazed at how your life will transform.

"Whatever the mind can conceive and believe, it can achieve."—Napoleon Hill

Have you considered where your beliefs came from? Did you intentionally devise a belief system using logic and reason? No, most likely you picked up your beliefs from your environment as you grew up. This is great news, isn't it? It means they are actually someone else's beliefs. He or she got those beliefs from other people, who got their beliefs from still other people! With this knowledge, you can let go of your limiting beliefs, and no longer accept them if they don't serve you well.

Here are a few beliefs you might never have questioned before, but they could be holding you back:

"Money doesn't buy happiness." (But neither does being broke.)

"My father said that nothing comes easily." (Have you ever noticed that people seem to do things the hard way?)

"You can't be successful if you don't go to college." (Many successful business owners did not graduate from college.)

There are many beliefs people have never questioned, assuming them to be true because they've heard other people voice them. Stop and think about it. Prejudices become instilled in people when they're young. As adults, they still haven't reconsidered those beliefs to form their own conclusions.

The mind is powerful. What you think about comes true and if you have limiting beliefs, you'll have limiting results. My friend Gerry Robert, who earned a six-figure income in his

20s, argued with a gentleman who told Gerry he could make $100,000 in a month. Gerry protested, saying why it couldn't and shouldn't happen. But then Gerry had a change of heart. He allowed himself to believe he could make even more money every month. And what happened? Within a year of that conversation, Gerry started making $100,000 a month. How many times have you been told to be realistic? What's realistic about making $100,000 a month? If Gerry fell for the "be realistic" belief, he wouldn't have achieved those spectacular results. In a few pages, you'll learn his system for programming your beliefs so you can achieve your dreams. (No peeking ahead!)

You might have heard the story about the belief that a mile couldn't be run in less than four minutes. Doctors, athletes, and other professionals said it wasn't possible. In 1954, a young man named Roger Banister proved them wrong. It only took 46 days before someone else broke his record. Within two years, more than 50 people did, and today, the number has risen into the thousands. How silly does it sound now that running a mile in less than four minutes can't be done?

"A man is but a product of his thought. What he thinks, he becomes."—Mahatma Gandhi

What you want is within your grasp. Have you ever noticed how some people with great opportunities have poor results and others who seemed to have few opportunities rise to greatness? The difference is rooted in their belief systems. Did you know that Michael Jordan was cut from his high school basketball team? If he had believed he wasn't any good, he might have quit forever and the game of basketball wouldn't bear his distinctive mark. Belief is the one thing that made all the difference.

Just as I pepper quotations throughout this book, you can use them to reinforce principles you believe in and even change your beliefs. You already have them in your head. Review this list of beliefs and see if you can identify any as belonging to you:

"I'm a failure."

"Nothing works."

"I'm not good enough."

"I'm not likeable."

"I wasn't meant to be happy."

"I'm so stupid."

"I can't do anything right."

"Something bad always happens to me."

Called victim language, this negative self-talk is poisonous because your subconscious, which doesn't know the difference between a truth and a lie, accepts these statements at face value and files them. The more you think these thoughts, the more your results will reflect them. The good news is that the same is true for positive thoughts. Research shows the average person thinks as many as 50,000 thoughts a day. How many of your thoughts are success-builders? How many are success-stealers?

You have the marvelous ability to reprogram yourself to have beliefs more congruent with what you want and who you want to be. You are the programmer. Consider all the thoughts you have. (Pretty deep, isn't it?) If a thought that's negative and self-defeating comes through, stop and tell yourself, "Cancel, cancel," then replace it with a positive thought. Doing this might feel silly at first, but the rewards will be worth it.

JANET'S STORY:
FROM LOW SELF-ESTEEM TO ENTREPRENEUR

"Ugly, inadequate, unattractive, worthless, insecure bitch—those were the names I'd attached to myself," says Janet. "I was my own worst enemy! I was my own greatest obstacle to overcome, especially my feelings of insecurity. I wallowed in the most negative thoughts about myself and believed everyone else was better than me. I wasn't even good enough to breathe."

Raised in "the Projects" in New York City, Janet was an only child whose perfectionist mother wanted the best for and from her daughter. Janet said, "I appreciate her for that because she brought out the best in me."

After high school, Janet worked as a secretary. Then, she said, "I married the wrong man because I was insecure." She was 23 when she began dating Jim. A year later, she married him, despite warnings from both her mother and even Jim's mother, who told Janet, "You're a nice girl. Jim's no good for you. You don't need to be with him. You deserve better."

But Janet thought "I wasn't attractive to other people, so when this tall, handsome man asked me to marry him, I felt I'd 'arrived.' I was so happy to be wanted."

Almost immediately, she realized her mistake. She had a handsome husband, but no love or support. After marrying Janet, Jim found a girlfriend with whom he had a baby. After that happened, Janet really felt like a failure, especially since her husband was verbally abusive and kept telling her she was the problem, which she believed. Janet's self-esteem reached its lowest ebb.

"I was unhappy," she remembers. "I woke up one Sunday morning and thought, I don't want this the rest of my life. I don't want to be with this guy who watches TV every Sunday, who doesn't want to do anything with his life, and who doesn't want me to do anything with mine."

Finally, Janet persuaded Jim to go to weekly marriage counseling sessions with her. "At the end of one session, the therapist asked to see me alone," Janet recalls. "Jim took that as a sign he'd been right about me being the problem."

However, Dr. Lillian Boone imparted a revelation. "When you're by yourself, you have a glow," the therapist said. "You light up a room. There's something very special about you."

"You mean I'm not the problem?"

"No, you're not the problem, Janet," Dr. Boone replied. "Without Jim, you're a different person. You're smart enough to do anything you want."

One night, after an argument during which Jim had once again called her "an insecure bitch," Janet started to cry. "Then I thought: Why am I crying? He's right. If I weren't insecure, I wouldn't be with him. I'm getting out of here. If Lillian said I can do it, I can. I'm leaving."

With the help of her mother and a friend, Janet packed her belongings, walked out, and never looked back. Her marriage had lasted for three and a half years.

Through counseling and reading books on self-improvement, Janet learned she was okay as she was. She gained confidence, realizing she was attractive and intelligent. Gradually, Janet shed the skin of low self-esteem.

One of the supervisors in Janet's office recognized her skills and competency and encouraged her to go to college. At the age of 30, she enrolled in college while working full time. Soon after, she realized it would take many years to finish her studies as a part-time student, so she quit her job, enrolled as a full-time student majoring in human resources, and found a part-time job.

After graduation, Janet was hired as a vice president of human resources at CitiBank, where she continued to acquire new skills and knowledge. Shortly before her 40th birthday, she realized she no longer found joy in her work. "I wanted a job that would make me want to get up in the morning," she says. "My life needed to be about more than just earning a paycheck." She turned to prayer, asking for enlightenment. "God told me to use my life skills and lessons to help other people believe in themselves and their dreams," Janet recalled.

With $10,000 in the bank, she quit her job and founded a non-profit organization called Vehicles in a tiny room at the Harlem YMCA. "I wanted to be the 'Vehicle' that bridged the gap between where my clients were and where they wanted to be," she says. To do this, Janet began providing life skills and career planning services.

"Once I started training clients, I realized that computer and typing skills were a small fraction of what they needed. They needed to learn how to live their lives, set goals, and relate to people," she says. "Using my life experiences, I developed strategies to help other people empower themselves to reach their goals and improve their lives."

Janet created courses to help clients believe in their own ability to do whatever they truly wanted to do. They served to boost their confidence through activities and tools that reinforced their innate capabilities. From there, they learned to develop a plan of action to realize their dreams.

"Vehicles doesn't operate like a program, but more like a training camp for clients' lives and careers," Janet explained. "First, we talk about what they like to do now and what they think they might like to do in the future. Then we offer assessments, provide character-building assignments, supply job training, send them on internships, and finally help them get jobs."

In its first eight years, Vehicles had more than 200 graduates. The organization currently employs 13 staff members. Through an active Board of Directors and Janet's never-ending persistence, Vehicles has established its own space in a church and has an annual operating budget of almost $1,000,000.

In 1997, Janet's achievements were recognized when she received the Avon Women of Enterprise Award, which honors leading U.S. female business owners from diverse industries and backgrounds for their entrepreneurial spirit and achievements.

LUPE'S STORY: FLOWING WITH LIFE'S CURVE BALLS

When Lupe was 11 years old, the Japanese military invaded her homeland. The residents in her Philippine village fled to the mountains, living in caves for many months. Gradually, they returned to their homes. Lupe's home, however, had been confiscated by the invading army, which was using it as a military barracks. Her father built a new house for his family near the school where he taught and the family settled into a life of hardship under the occupying forces. Wary of any public gatherings, the Japanese rulers initially wouldn't even allow children to attend school. Later, they forced the children to attend school to study Japanese.

Lupe's family and others in her village hid Philippine soldiers who had refused to surrender to the Japanese. They shared their food and supplies with these resistance fighters until the American military parachuted in provisions for them.

She harbors harsh memories of the war. "Three of my cousins went to the war as junior officers, and when they came home, they looked like skeletons. One of them had been tortured by the Japanese. Not only did I hear terrible stories of atrocities from my cousins and resistance fighters, I also caught glimpses with my own eyes of Japanese soldiers torturing captives when I walked past their compound."

As the war progressed, bombings by both Japanese and American forces destroyed most of Lupe's village. "When General MacArthur and the Americans returned," she recalled, "our original house was one of only two that hadn't been destroyed by Japanese or American bombs.

"My experiences during the war shaped my destiny. I wanted to help others who'd been affected by war," Lupe said. "Although I was educated as a teacher, I kept becoming involved with social work because of my family's commitment to others. I taught college, then worked in the Office of Vocational Rehabilitation. While attending school to get a master's degree in education, I decided to go to Vietnam. The U.S. Commerce Department had set up a relief organization to help Vietnamese refugees. I joined this organization and worked in a vocational rehabilitation center with veterans who had disabilities."

When she was in her late 20's, Lupe came to the United States to participate in a work-study program in social work at the University of Pennsylvania in Philadelphia. During this time, she worked with delinquent children and elderly people. She also met and married her husband, Carl.

In the early 1960's, the couple moved to Arizona for Carl's health. Lupe found a position as a hospital social worker but had to quit when her husband became very ill. She needed to earn a living and also be at home to take care of Carl so she turned to a skill she had acquired in home economics classes—sewing. Slowly, through word of mouth, she supported herself and Carl by creating clothing for local women and designing costumes for a small theater company.

Although Lupe continued to support Carl until his death in 1972, the couple separated in 1967 and Lupe moved to New York City. She lived with a friend until she was earning enough money to find her own apartment. She enrolled at the Fashion Institute of Technology, learning pattern-making and other design skills. While studying, Lupe worked in New York's Garment District and acquired private clients. After graduation, she slowly built her private business.

Lupe sent money home to help members of her family in the Philippines where the Marcos regime had made life very difficult. After her parents died, she paid for her siblings to join her in New York—first her oldest sister, then four brothers and their wives. Each time, the new arrivals lived with Lupe until they found work and moved into their own homes. She still provides financial help for some of her relatives in America as well as in the Philippines, and one day hopes to bring her nieces and nephews to the United States.

Around the time Carl died, Lupe developed problems with one eye, which led her to study alternative medicine and many healing traditions, including Reiki. The problems worsened—she eventually lost sight in one eye—forcing Lupe to stop working in the fashion industry.

Lupe then turned to another love of hers – being a spiritual healer. "I began the healing journey not in a religious way but in a way that works with light. Light is where we come from and where we go back to. I want to be a light to all my family members—to help them be what they want to be.

"I know I can help people get over their miseries, whatever they are. Everything I ever studied is helping me, including my training in nutrition. I use a combination of systems that work together—higher energy, spirituality, and bodywork. Healing is a combination of the physical, mental, and spiritual. I can heal physically without interfering with a client's relationship with the medical profession."

When asked how she's managed to keep going through her hardships and challenges, Lupe said, "It was all hard, but I was lucky. Whatever I felt determined to do, I eventually completed it because I believed in myself. As a family, our goal has always been to not be dependent on anyone, but to help. That's how we were raised.

"There are so many things I still want to do. My biggest achievement would be to put into the heads of the younger ones that life is about more than just yourself. It's all about helping humanity. If you're useful to others, you're achieving something because you're not disturbing the natural flow of life. Eventually we go back to the point from which we came. In the meantime, do what you believe is right and don't hurt those around you."

KEY STRATEGY TO INSTILL BELIEF IN YOURSELF

You're about to learn an incredible tool to reprogram your subconscious mind. Gerry Robert's Captain and Crew concept from his book *The Millionaire Mindset* is based on the premise that you are the "captain" and your subconscious mind is the "crew." Whatever you say or think, your crew will respond, "Okay," and take it as an order. So be careful what you say and think. "I'm so tired," or "You're driving me nuts," or "I never get anything done," and other seemingly innocent thoughts will manifest as your crew goes to work to make them true.

This simple tool could turn your life around by helping you change your limiting beliefs to achieve your goals and dreams. It's been used, in various forms, for centuries to alter people's lives and what is attracted to them. Think big. (Refer to pages 26 to 31 of *The Millionaire Mindset* for more details.)

Here's how to use this tool:

1. Make a list of whatever your heart desires.

Don't worry about whether you can afford the items you list, know how to get them, or see any obstacles in the way. Just list what you want in answer to the question "What would you like to have, do, or be?" Write everything in the present tense, as if you already possess what you desire. Write out all your desires for each area of life. (Emotional, spiritual, vocational, physical, relational, travel, material. Be balanced. Write it all.)

2. Write out the list in your own handwriting.

Because people think in pictures, this exercise requires you to imagine what you earnestly desire. Don't fret about "how" these things will come to you. Your job is simply to hold the image.

3. Start each day by rewriting your Heart's Desire list.

Use a new sheet to rewrite the items on your list each day. Don't photocopy it—it must be written in your handwriting. You need to convince your crew (your subconscious mind) that you seriously desire what you've written down. It will interpret them as commands from you (the captain) and respond with the only word it knows, "Yes." Then it uses the Law of Attraction to produce those images in your life. Personal development leader Bob Proctor has said, "The mind is a powerful magnet and as such attracts whatever corresponds to its ruling state."

4. Carry your Heart's Desire list with you at all times.

Find a special place to carry this list. Men might reserve their front pants pocket for carrying this list; women could find a similar place. Put nothing else in that place and always carry it with you. *Always!* Never change its location. Keep it loose and on its own, not with other items like a wallet. Touch the sheet of paper several times a day so what you've written pops onto the screen of your mind frequently. The more you do this ritual, the more you attract the images of what you want into your life. Feel free to keep the sheets once you've attained a particular item on it; it's a good reminder of the power you and your crew have.

5. Identify your A-1 goal.

What one goal from the list stands out as the most important or the one you're most passionate about? This is you're

A-1 goal. Once you've folded the sheet to fit in your pocket, write it on the outside of the sheet. This focuses you even more.

Make several copies of the format page that follows, using one for each day. Place a fresh one on your desk as you leave the office every day. Start every day by training your crew. If you do this for 90 days, your life will change the way you want it to!

MEMORANDUM

To: The Crew   **Date:** _____

From: The Captain   **Re: My Heart's Desire**

Message: Make this happen!

"I'm so happy now that...

_____

_____

_____

_____

_____

_____

_____

_____

_____

_____

_____

_____

Signature

(Used with permission. Gerry Robert, *The Millionaire Mindset*)

"The only thing that can grow is the thing you give energy to; and energy flows to where the concentration goes." —Gerry Robert

Chapter 3

I Can See Clearly Now: Removing Roadblocks of Fear

"Do what you fear and your fear will die."
—Ralph Waldo Emerson

I'll never forget the first time I got behind the wheel of a car. I was 29 years old and petrified. With hands dripping sweat and tears rolling down my face, I gripped the wheel so hard my palms turned red.

Why put myself through this anxiety? Well, I'd moved from a big city with abundant public transportation to an area with none. I had two choices: drive or starve. I even found a driver education school that assisted nervous drivers. Finally, I found an instructor who put me at ease and forced me to let go of my fear. My life in my new environment depended on it. I gritted my teeth, prayed, and finally learned to drive.

Sheri Sharman was once a shy young lady who would walk home for lunch because she was afraid of entering the high school cafeteria alone. In speech class, she refused to give a speech because she was so afraid of what her classmates would think, even though she knew the teacher wouldn't fail her. Yet, she went on to graduate and teach preschool. Later, she changed careers and found herself in the relationship business. The more people she helped, the more money she made. She did so well, in fact, that one day, she was chosen to speak in front of thousands of people. Given only one day's notice, she felt petrified, but she did it. Today, more than 30 years later, she makes millions of dollars as a public speaker. She's spoken in stadiums filled with tens of thousands of people as well as to small groups of women. She loves to help people empower themselves to conquer their biggest fears like she did. As she put it, "I turned my biggest fear into my career."

> "I have not ceased being fearful, but I have ceased to let fear control me."—Erica Jong

How to Conquer Fear

Have you ever overcome a fear like she did? It's powerful! The fear of public speaking is known to rank as the number one fear, followed by the fear of darkness, the fear of being alone, the fear of a wasted life, the fear of making a mistake, the fear of looking foolish, the fear of rejection, and on and on.

By addressing your fears and restoring your inner balance, you'll gain the resilience and healthy outlook you need to get through difficult times. Your thoughts play a huge part in this. I suggest you focus on which thoughts are fear-based, then "correct" them to eliminate your fear. For example, the thought "Why would he go out with me?" is corrected to "He might go out with me." More importantly, take action in spite of your fears. People often think they'll take action when their fear goes away. Yet successful people decide to take action *in spite of* their fears. You can, too.

Sometimes, people's feelings about themselves play a role in fear. If you don't feel "good enough," then naturally, you might fear success or recognition. If you do feel "good enough," those fears diminish or disappear. It can go the other way, too. The more fears you give attention to in your thoughts, the worse you might feel about yourself.

JUST DO IT

Author Susan Jeffers said it all when she said, "Feel the fear and do it anyway." That's easier said than done. It requires a commitment to train yourself to just do it.

Babies are born with only two fears: falling and loud noises. Every other fear gets programmed into them. That indicates you have the power to change that programming and take total control over them. You don't have to depend on anyone else to do it for you. Once you understand that fear is thought-based and belief-based, you simply decide which thoughts and beliefs no longer serve you, and you dismantle them.

It's impossible to be afraid of something while in the middle of doing what you're afraid of. Let's consider the number-one fear— public speaking. If you're on the podium in front of a crowd talking, gesturing, smiling, connecting, you can no longer be afraid of it. You might feel nervous, but you aren't afraid of doing it because you *are* doing it.

Miraculous things happen to those who consciously choose to overcome their fears. As you move forward, your inner strengths will emerge. You'll gain confidence in your skills, abilities, and even your downfalls. You'll learn more about yourself, your wants, needs, and desires, thus opening new doors of opportunity and enjoyment.

"You gain strength, courage, and confidence in every experience in which you stop and look fear in the face. You must do the thing you cannot do."
—Eleanor Roosevelt

When you remove the shackles that held you, you'll hit the high notes of life expressed in Johnny Nash's song "I Can See Clearly Now." There will be "nothin' but blue skies" after you remove "all obstacles in my way" and "all the dark clouds that had me blind" before you see "the rainbow I've been prayin' for." As you begin to see the world as "a bright, bright sun shiny day," you'll end your long history of self-sabotage to live the life you so richly deserve.

It's time to turn on the light and step through the door of empowerment. Behold, a brilliant new "sun shiny" day!

HILDA: CHOOSING LIFE ONE DAY AT A TIME

"From birth until I was 18 years old, I don't remember a day I breathed freely or didn't hold fear and death foremost in my mind. I don't remember a single moment of joy," said a young woman named Hilda.

Of Mexican and Yaqui Indian heritage, Hilda had moved with her family from a small Mexican town where only Spanish was spoken to Ajo, a copper-mining town of about 6,000 people in the Sonoran desert of southern Arizona. Hilda's father worked for the Phelps-Dodge Corporation at its huge open pit mine near Ajo. At night, he played drums in a band that performed at local bars.

The mining company provided most of the houses in Ajo, which was segregated into three distinct areas. The Anglo engineers and managers lived in the nicest homes in the hills. The Native Americans lived on the other side of town—the poorest section of town—up against the open pit. And the Mexican laborers lived down the hillside from the Anglos, closer to the smelter and tailings area of the mine.

Hilda's family lived in the Mexican area in a house that had three rooms with a tiny bathroom off the bedroom in which the entire family slept. Hilda remembered growing up in this small house as "an unending battlefield" where her mother, she, and three siblings perpetually expected beatings and verbal abuse from their alcoholic husband and father.

"Father needed to control everything, including allowing us only a limited time to play with our friends," Hilda recalled. "He didn't like us to have other children in our home—it was too disruptive for him. And he didn't want us involved in any activities that he couldn't control. So we spent most of our days anticipating when he would leave for work and dreading the moment he would come home."

The only caring words Hilda ever heard from her father were uttered when she nearly died from severe hemorrhaging at age six. Waking up in a hospital room with life support equipment attached to her body, Hilda remembered being surrounded by her parents and a priest. "My father cried loudly and uncontrollably. He called my name over and over, begging me not to leave. I watched, hovering above the scene."

In his anguish, he pleaded with God to save his daughter. Hilda listened as he cried and promised, "Please God, let her live! I'll change my life for the better!" Hilda sensed a voice saying to her, "Look down and see what's happening. Do you want to stay with them, or would you like to leave now? It's your choice." Believing the promises her father made to God, she chose life.

When at last she got well enough to go home, Hilda waited all day for her father to return from work. "As soon as he walked in the kitchen door, I ran to him and threw my arms around his waist," she recalled. But her father's anger pushed her away and devastated Hilda. He shouted, "Get away from me! You're no longer my daughter. You don't have my blood. You're not my child any more!" You see, Hilda had an unusual blood type and the transfusions that had saved her life came from blood donated by an Anglo man.

Realizing that her father was lying about his promise to God engulfed Hilda in fear. Not surprisingly, it didn't take long for the drinking, yelling, and beatings to begin again.

Being at school offered no respite. Although about 70 percent of the students were of Mexican heritage, the nuns spoke only English and insisted the children do likewise. "We were told never to speak our native language," Hilda says, "and to forget that we were anything but Americans. In the name of God, the nuns were going to beat English and some sense into us."

Abused at home and at school, Hilda said, "I lost my childhood to terror, restraints, and demands that left deep fears and emotional scars."

Two days after graduating from high school, she moved to Phoenix with her sister Maggie and two friends. The girls rented a small apartment, the nicest place Hilda had ever lived. When her companions returned to Ajo, Hilda stayed alone in Arizona's capital city. As frightening as this was, it felt safer than what the 18-year-old girl had left behind. She decided never to live in her parents' home again.

While working three jobs to support herself, Hilda enrolled in a cosmetology training program. There, for the first time, she experienced kindness. Several people befriended her and helped her remove the shell of shame and isolation she'd built around herself.

Graduating in record time, Hilda got her first professional job in a busy hairdressing salon. Her life was changing for the better. Then at age 19, she was diagnosed with cervical cancer. She endured repeated surgeries, never telling her family about the illness because she didn't want her mother to worry.

Hilda's desire to feel loved and safe led her to marry a needy man 14 years older than her. To add to her burdens, he spent most of his time traveling on business, leaving Hilda to care for his mother who was dying. Her mother-in-law made no effort to hide the resentment she felt toward Hilda.

Yearning for someone to love, Hilda wanted to have a child. Her medical condition posed serious risks, but in spite of warnings from her doctor, Hilda chose to become pregnant. With great joy, she gave birth to a healthy boy. But her happiness was tempered by her discovery that the cervical cancer had spread, so she had a hysterectomy. At age 22, she seemed doomed to a life of crises.

Hilda had the primary responsibility of caring for both her young son and her dying mother-in-law, in addition to working in the salon several days a week. Although she seemed to be coping, she developed several neurotic behaviors, including anorexia and compulsively scrubbing and scouring her house.

Enduring six years of marriage, Hilda realized she had to break away and divorce her husband, even though he shared a strong bond with their son. After her marriage ended, she learned that her ex-husband was depressed and didn't love her. A year after her divorce, Hilda married a talented, charismatic, and energetic man named Jerry. He appeared to be everything she wanted to be *herself* but felt too insecure to become that person on her own. In her naiveté and unending desire to feel loved, safe, and secure, Hilda was blinded to another side of her husband's personality. Diagnosed as manic-depressive, his illness controlled their lives.

Hilda compared this relationship to being on a roller coaster. "It was a frightening ride with no seatbelts to hold me or my son. During his highs, Jerry showered me with gifts, but his lows consisted of rising debts, verbal abuse, and total lack of control. I felt the familiar terror of my childhood all over again."

The couple separated but reunited when Jerry promised

to work out his problems. They bought a big house, which was like a dream come true for this little Indian/Mexican girl from Ajo. Hilda said, "I believed I had everything."

Jerry, however, was living beyond his means. When the couple separated a second time, he didn't pay the mortgage, so the Indian tribe repossessed their house. He also hadn't paid the couple's income taxes, forcing Hilda to file for bankruptcy and sell everything to pay off bills, taxes, and attorney's fees. Ill again, Hilda developed severe panic attacks. "I didn't believe I deserved to be happy. I didn't know what happiness felt like," she said.

In desperation, Hilda wrote a letter to her son asking for his forgiveness, then took all the tranquilizers prescribed for her panic attacks and depression. "I went to sleep ready to die. It would soon all be over. At last I'd have some peace."

Sometime before sunrise Hilda awoke. "I was alive! I'd been given the gift of life," she said. "At that moment I knew my life would change, and that I was the only one who could make it happen."

Following this epiphany, Hilda recalled, "God became my partner and I set out to discover my true and whole self. I prayed for wisdom, guidance, and strength. I committed myself to become consciously alive for the first time in my life. This started my journey to the other side of fear and terror."

Hilda's quest for self-knowledge led her to holistic medicine and intensive therapy. "I realized change had to come from within before I could create it on the outside," she said. "I consciously paid attention to every thought and became acutely aware of my environment and the people I allowed in it. When I was ready to learn, the right teachers appeared. Through therapy, I learned that physical illness helped me avoid the emotional turmoil of my life. Slowly the pieces of the puzzle came together."

Hilda found "a spiritual home" in the teachings of Science of Mind through the Church of Religious Science. "Through this church, I moved from dark to light, from fear to love. I embraced the spirit and developed a passionate desire to help others discover themselves and reclaim their lives, too."

Hilda finally developed within herself the security and safety she'd tried so desperately to find through other people. Today, she's an ordained minister, teacher, and workshop facilitator who addresses important aspects of life's journey: living beyond fear, taking risks, creating abundance, and developing spiritually. A gifted speaker, she shares her personal experiences with perspective and humor.

Hilda also owns a successful hairstyling salon and founded the non-profit organization Vision Gatherings, Inc., a spiritual and professional organization for women. In addition, she's president of Pluma Publishing, Inc., a company that publishes spiritual books and other inspirational material. Her first book, *Living on the Other Side of Fear*, tells about her own healing journey from a childhood of hardship and fear to a life of abundance and love.

Incorporating her Mexican and Yaqui Indian heritage with her love and respect for all people, Hilda teaches: "We are one in thought, one in creative emotions, and one in every relationship."

KEY STRATEGIES FOR OVERCOMING FEAR

Now it's your turn.

- Write down all your fears. Go over each one and write one way you can combat each fear.
- Make a list of positive affirmations that help combat those fears. (For example, if you have a fear of being alone, write: I am happy and safe in my home.)
- Burn the piece of paper with your fears on it. Watch

it burn and think about releasing your fears.

- Each day, do something you're afraid of. Take baby steps. Celebrate your successes.
- Seek others who have overcome the fears you have. Talk with them and ask for their support.

Chapter 4

If I Were Brave: Bouncing Back

"Forget past mistakes. Forget failures. Forget about everything except what you're going to do now— and do it." —William Durant

You've likely exhibited resilience at some point in your life, especially during your childhood. Children can be brave because as they go through rough situations, they don't know that they're "rough." They don't know the difference as an adult does. Adults are often amazed at children's resilience. I'm sure that if you think back on your life, you can remember times when you're not even sure how you made it through particular situations. This is when resilience and bravery kicked in and you forged ahead.

An increasing body of research from fields of psychology, psychiatry, and sociology is showing that most people, including young people, can bounce back from risks, stress, and trauma. They go on to experience success in life, rebounding from difficult situations with more power and wisdom.

Be grateful for the problems from which you've bounced back because they gave you the strength you have today and built your character. The worse your problems are, the stronger you can become. As the expression goes, "That which doesn't kill us makes us stronger."

Often there's a story of bravery behind successful people. I absolutely love Oprah Winfrey's story. Of all the successful women in the world, she's the one I'd most love to meet. Her persistence, bravery, and stamina have given me hope and encouraged me to reach for success.

Thank goodness Thomas Edison was persistent about working on the light bulb. He didn't get it to work until after his 10,000th try. To him, that meant he simply found 10,000 ways that it didn't work first.

Harland Sanders had to learn to cook after his father died when Harland was six years old. He started Kentucky Fried Chicken at age 65 with his first social security check of $105. It has been said that he talked to more than a thousand people before his recipe finally caught on. Resilience? You bet!

After reading those examples, you might think you can't rise to success if you haven't had something bad happen to you. Don't despair. You've probably overcome more than you think. Besides, if you have a burning desire to reach a goal, it doesn't matter what your background is.

A NEW PERSPECTIVE ON CHALLENGES

Bravery and resilience give you a new perspective on challenges. At some point in your life, you've probably thought to yourself, "I've been through worse. I can make it through this." Your experiences and resulting bravery are key to facing future problems and helping others with theirs. You can't always tell others what to do, but you can share your experiences and give people hope.

Help from family and friends bolsters bravery. A special bond is forged when you go through tough times with people you love—and even people you dislike. Misery loves company and it also forges bonds. Many support groups have been formed by people who share a similar negative experience, such as the death of a loved one, alcohol or drug abuse, miscarriage or abortion, suicide of a loved one, abuse survivors, and many others.

As with all the strategies in this book, your ability to bounce back helps build self-confidence. Give yourself a pat on the back. You're still here. It would be impossible for you to be here unless you had made it through to the other side of your past difficulties.

VERA'S STORY: LETTING TIME DO WHAT TIME DOES BEST

"I've been watching you for the past six months. You will have a significant impact in this world. I know you're meant for greatness and I'm going to nurture and guide you."

This statement came from Kate Patterson, Vera's foster mother, a woman who never completed eighth grade. She made that statement when Vera was only 11 years old.

Vera, along with her four biological siblings, had been taken away from her natural mother when she was nine. State officials had deemed this mother unfit to take care of her children. At first, the children were cared for by Mr. and Mrs. Brown in a small place called Egg Harbor. Vera remembers happy times in the country with the Browns, even though their rustic home had no electricity or indoor plumbing.

Vera clearly recalls the day in June, 1954, when she turned 11. That's when she and two of her siblings were taken to live with a new foster mother, Kate Patterson, in Atlantic City, New Jersey. She remembers her surprise in finding two sheets on each of the beds—thinking that was a mistake. She had only seen one sheet on beds during her whole life.

It was Kate Patterson who recognized Vera's intelligence and exceptionality, so she coached, groomed, and molded this young woman for an important role in life—being a strong black woman. Kate took her role seriously and followed through on her promise to nurture her foster daughter's self-esteem.

This show of confidence in Vera's abilities marked the first time anyone had told her she was special, or that she could have a positive impact on the lives of others. These messages from her "mom" instilled such confidence and pride in Vera that when she graduated from high school she had the second highest marks in her class. This prepared her well for secretarial positions in the workplace as well as for continued academic studies.

After graduation, Vera planned to get a job but changed her mind when one of her teachers, Josephine Turner, intervened. Ms. Turner told her that anyone with such good grades and standing should consider going to college. So she helped Vera apply to Trenton State College, where she received a full work scholarship and began with a major in education. Vera's strong typing skills prepared her for a position as secretary to the chairman of the Art Department—a job she kept all four years at Trenton.

Vera's early nurturing and self-confidence aided her more than two decades later when she faced one of the biggest decisions of her life: Should she divorce her husband of 16 years? She and her husband Bill lived in Greenwich, Connecticut, in a middle-class neighborhood. Though he had worked in the corporate world for many years, he was one of the first employees let go when his company began downsizing.

Before the lay-off in 1984, he was a happy, easy-going person. But after, he behaved so differently that Vera hardly knew him. Bill harbored a lot of resentment. After spending so many years in college, he had achieved the ultimate American dream for a black man—working in corporate America. To earn the respect of the white men around him, he worked twice as hard as they did, staying at the office and taking numerous business trips away from family.

Unfortunately, Bill had attached his self-esteem and

confidence—his whole world—to his job. He let it become the center of his life. Yet his dedication was for nothing, for he was left with no job, and therefore no identity.

For months, he tried to find another high-paying job. Due to his impressive résumé, he was called for several interviews, but no job panned out. During this time, he started a business, which failed dismally. This added to his frustration and diminished his self-esteem even more.

Year after year, he wallowed in self-pity and began to lash out at those closest to him. His feelings of devastation and shame began to take a toll on Vera and their sons.

Finally, Vera had had enough. She faced a crossroad in her life: She could leave him, get a divorce, and move on. Or she could try to make the marriage work.

As a successful motivational speaker, Vera had proven she could make a living on her own. Her career was on an upswing and she was traveling a lot, speaking to groups and leading workshops. She knew she was capable of caring for herself and her children since she had already taken on the financial responsibilities of her family. In fact, because of her increased income, their lifestyle didn't change after her husband lost his job.

So why should she put up with this less-than-loving behavior from her spouse? She prayed and dug deep—deep into her soul, into the character Kate had built inside her, into her own resilience. She analyzed all the lessons she taught in her seminars and applied them to herself. Then she harnessed her strength and reserves.

Vera remembered that, as a youngster, all the other children on her block had their parents' name. But her last name was different than Kate's. When she told her mother about feeling insecure because of this, Kate said, "You could let that slow you down or you could let that light you up. You have a choice."

Vera used this lesson to help her decide how to make a decision about her marriage. She realized she had a choice. So she confronted Bill and said, "I'm tired of this wallowing in self-pity. You can get on the train with your family or you can choose to remain behind."

As fragile as he was, he chose to "get on the train" by becoming a silent but participating member of the family while he worked through his issues. At the same time, Vera decided to "reset her binoculars" to change her own perceptions about the situation.

This helped her understand where her husband was coming from. She acknowledged that, at this time, he wasn't capable of doing better. She lovingly drew a big imaginary circle around him and spread a spiritual blanket over him. Then she gave up trying to control the situation or his life. Simply stated, she stopped expecting from him what he couldn't give.

Next, she asked herself, "What do I really want?" The answer came to her loud and clear: "I want to stay married." She had invested a lot in the relationship; they had two sons who needed a father; she had much to be grateful for. In addition, her husband had been the impetus behind the success of her business. Inherently a decent man, he continued to care about her and his sons despite his difficulties.

Something else very important happened. Vera stopped being afraid of the future. Instead, she focused on their life together in the present. At the same time, she brought back many fond memories—like when he had taken her shopping at the mall with his very first paycheck. They barely knew each other then. Yet even after 30 years, she recalled the beautiful blue raincoat, umbrella, and galoshes he bought for her that day. She also remembered the beautiful, thoughtful cards he had given her on special occasions—and continued to do so.

Still, despite her courageous decision, it was not easy to remain in this relationship. Many times, she doubted she could go on. But she nurtured her deep faith in God and learned the lesson of humility. In the beginning, she took several steps forward and some backward. She remained committed to her decision and kept focusing on love and respect.

Things changed very little for Bill. But as the years rolled by, he stopped feeling sorry for himself and continued to pursue leads in the classified ads. Vera learned to understand she could not change him—she could only change herself.

Today, Vera and Bill are best friends and accept each other "as is." He has continued to be the wind beneath her sails, encouraging, coaching, and helping her in her business, even assisting in some projects she wouldn't have taken on without his help.

Through all this, Vera has realized she can't treat a relationship like a styrofoam cup that gets discarded when the juice is gone. It's essential to look at oneself and alter any expectations that get in the way of accepting others.

"Let time do what time does best," she advises, "and use that time to become comfortable with yourself, make good choices for yourself, and rejoice in your accomplishments."

Chances are, she heard Kate give that same advice many decades ago.

MERCEDES: REDEFINING AN IDENTITY

Mercedes met Ron when they were both 13 years old. They dated for five years and she married him when she was 18. Her parents were extremely disappointed when she quit college after her first year. Wanting the perfect family, she devoted herself to becoming the perfect mother and wife.

Mercedes's life changed dramatically with one phone call in the wee hours of the morning in early May, 1989. The voice on the phone said words that she would never forget. "There has been an accident. Come to the hospital immediately, bring someone with you, and don't bring the children." Petrified, panic-stricken, and fearing the worst, she threw on some clothes as her mind raced with worries. She called her sister and arranged for the care of her two children, Brian and John, aged four and six. In a state of panic and fear, she frantically drove to the hospital.

Running up the hospital steps, she moved in a trance-like state as though she was being gently pushed. She felt in her bones that she was about to hear really bad news. A woman met her at the entrance and guided her to her husband's room. Gingerly, she drew open the curtains surrounding his bed and saw something that would remain imprinted in her memory forever.

Her husband lay there, hooked up to every machine possible with wires going into every part of his body. She could hardly see his face or recognize him. She searched for the only thing that would indicate hope: the heart monitor's jagged lines. But the red line was flat and straight. That's when she realized her husband was dead.

Her darkest fear confirmed, she gasped in horror and lost control. Her screams could be heard all over the hospital as she came to grips with this horror. This was the man she had just said good-bye to the previous day. This was the man who had left home to attend a stag party for his best friend. This just couldn't be *him*!

For the next few days, in a state of numbness and total shock, Mercedes went through the motions of funeral planning. There was no time for immediate grief or crying; she had to get into gear and arrange all the details, notify his family and friends, order the flowers, select the casket, take care of the funeral arrangements, and order food for those who would come to the house after the funeral.

His family didn't offer any financial help or emotional support. Thankfully, her family helped with the finances since she had no money. This was her first experience with death and she had to adjust fast. So she called on an angel – an angel who had saved her once before when she was a child. When she was five years old, she had nearly drowned, but the wings of that angel had brought her back to the surface of the water. She still remembered watching the other children jumping into the pool, and even though she didn't know how to swim, she jumped into the deep end. She couldn't come up to the surface. As she struggled to breathe, she felt someone with outstretched arms pushing her up. That someone, she believed, was an angel. This incident helped form her strong spiritual beliefs and gave her faith that she would never be left alone. Despite the daze she was experiencing with the tragedy of her husband's death, she moved through the aftermath with faith and assurance that the same angel was holding her up.

As the numbness wore off and reality hit months later, little by little, she began to accept her loss. She had to confront the difficult reality that someone she had lived with would never be physically present to her again.

Her grief was compounded by the absence of answers about his death. The death certificate read "overdose" but no one, not even his best friend who had quietly dropped him off at the hospital, would give any explanation of what really happened. Adding to the puzzle was the fact that her husband was a medical student and a severe asthmatic. Those questions remained unanswered even 12 years after his death.

Mercedes realized that her identity had been idealistically formed through her role with her husband and children. Because she was no longer a wife, she had to redefine herself. Her widowhood status was compounded by a lack of income, which had become her greatest problem. She neither had money nor insurance—in short, she had no security. How would she take care of herself and her two children? She had never asked questions concerning insurance or money; they had never discussed arrangements if anything happened to him. Being young, they thought life would go on forever.

As Mercedes began to reconstruct and recapture her true self, she discovered who she really was—a strong, determined, deeply spiritual human being. She decided she couldn't dwell on the past, but needed to forge into the future, so she dug deep to discover what she really loved to do. As a child, she remembered she loved to style hair for her friends and put on makeup. She remembered the joy and pleasure they expressed about feeling transformed at her hands. She decided to pursue this interest and talent and attend cosmetology school. Once she graduated, she worked at one of the top spas in the area and developed a long running list of clients who loved her work. At one point a few years later, she decided to open her own salon. "It's going to happen! I've paid my dues and one day I'll have my place. I'm ready and am not afraid."

Today, Mercedes is the proud owner of "Mercedes," a salon in an upscale, affluent community. She has truly come full circle in the process of healing and redefining her identity.

CYNTHIA INABINETT'S STORY:
UNCOVERING THE REAL PERSON

Cynthia dropped out of school at the early age of 15 after completing 8th grade. At the time, she got pregnant by a man nine years her senior. One year later, she fell in love with tall, charming, friendly Robert who was seven years older than her. They wanted to get married. He dressed well and really did seem to care for her and her child. Since Cynthia was underage, her mother had to give her permission for the marriage to happen. Cynthia knew nothing about him or his family except that he worked at the post office. She married him because she was "in love, had a young child, and wanted to get away from a crowded household." Unfortunately, he couldn't afford an apartment, so they lived with her mother and five younger siblings, sleeping on the foldout couch in a cramped apartment.

Six months after the wedding, Cynthia's mother died suddenly. She had gotten up that morning and did what she always did: made a big pot of oatmeal and put it on the table. The next thing Cynthia knew, her mother had fallen on the kitchen floor. Although she was rushed to the hospital, it was too late. She had had a massive stroke and never regained consciousness. She died the next day.

Cynthia went into a state of shock after her mother was buried. Not only did she lose her mother, but she also lost her younger siblings—Reda, 14, Diane, 13, Gene, 12, Peaches, 10, and Tyrone, 8—who were all sent to live with relatives. Cynthia thought that since she was married, she'd legally be able to take care of her five siblings; however the state felt that at age 16, Cynthia was too young to care for them. With tears in her eyes and a broken heart, she watched as they were taken away.

The landlord allowed what was left of her family to remain in the apartment until the end of the month, but then they had to move because they couldn't afford the rent. The double loss and the move were unbearable for a grieving Cynthia. Her mother, who was her sole supporter, was gone, her younger siblings were gone, her older siblings were living their own lives elsewhere, and no one could offer her the comfort she needed. She felt completely abandoned. She had no one to go to for solace, to hear her cries of sorrow. What she did have was a husband who had suddenly turned hostile, feeling the pressure of being the sole supporter. He resented the burden of being responsible for a grieving wife and child who was not his own.

They moved into a small one-room apartment that turned into hell in every sense of the word. Violence and abuse erupted on a daily basis. Cynthia lived with her angry, violent husband through three years of physical and mental abuse. It reminded her of the pushing, hitting, and slapping she saw between her parents as a child. But she thought it was natural for husbands and wives to fight, so she accepted their frequent fights as normal.

Still, any small thing triggered her husband's uncontrollable temper. She later learned his moodiness stemmed from drug use. The signs of drug abuse were there earlier, but Cynthia didn't recognize them. She said, "I saw white, powdery stuff around and sometimes threw it out, not knowing it was coke."

She recalled a time she was coming home, laden down with groceries, and a male neighbor offered to help her bring them up the many flights of stairs. He had placed the groceries on the table and was about to leave when her husband walked in. After he left, her husband flew into a jealous rage—ranting and screaming every profanity under the sun. He accused her of having an affair and demanded to know why the neighbor was in the house. In this uncontrollable rage, he was deaf to any explanations.

Many times, her husband came home late at night from work and would sleep until late in the morning. One morning, her son Barry woke up crying. She tried feeding him his bottle, but he wouldn't stop crying no matter what she did. Suddenly, her husband jumped out of bed, grabbed the baby out of her arms, and began beating him. The harder he cried, the harder he hit him. Finally, when Cynthia could take it no more, she grabbed a mayonnaise jar and hit her husband in the head.

She snatched the baby from him and ran out the door, leaving her husband bleeding profusely.

Two months later, Cynthia discovered she was pregnant. She wasn't happy about the pregnancy, yet secretly and naively thought that a child of his own would make a difference in their relationship. But this news didn't stop the violence; in fact, the arguments grew worse and the fights became more brutal. He taught her to fear him. Many times, she ended up in the emergency room with black eyes and stomach pains. "It's a miracle that the baby wasn't harmed during these episodes," she said.

Cynthia continued fighting for her life because it was her only way of surviving. She cried in the dark for her mother. "How can I get away from this hell?" she asked herself. "It's impossible for me to live like this." She planned many escapes, but all her attempts failed. Not feeling confident that she could support herself and her children, she stayed in the apartment waiting for the right moment to leave. One time, she had packed everything to walk out before he came home, but when the planned time arrived, he came home early.

On another occasion, after she had prepared a meal for him, he just looked at her and punched her square in the eye. As blood gushed from an open cut, he stood and watched her, completely defenseless and wailing from the pain. She still bears the scar over her eye. Her small children watched in horror as he inflicted pain on a regular basis.

Finally, Cynthia could take it no more; she had to escape from this insanity before he actually killed her. He suspected that she was planning to leave and dealt the final assault. He met her at her job and demanded that she get into the taxi cab with him. When she refused, he proceeded to hit her over the head with the butt end of a knife, kicking her, dragging her, pulling, screaming, and yelling. As he dragged her across the street, all she could see was blood, which blinded her sight as pain ripped through her battered and bruised body. People in the street witnessed this assault and did nothing. As she screamed for help, they continued minding their own business.

Finally, when his strength was spent, he walked away leaving her for dead. Mustering all her strength, she dragged her beaten and broken body to a police station several blocks away. She fell in the doorway and blacked out. Cynthia remained in a coma for more than two days, hovering between life and death. When she finally regained consciousness and opened her eyes, she found her sister Marie at her side. Marie had been called as the next of kin. She remained at Cynthia's side day and night until she was released from the hospital. Marie nursed and cared for her like the mother she had lost three years before. When she asked about her children, she was told that her husband had taken their child and disappeared, and that he had left three-year-old Barry playing in the street alone. Marie had found him and took him to her house. Marie had no idea that Cynthia was being abused. Cynthia had never told anyone because she felt so ashamed.

The detectives questioned her about her husband's background. They asked where she thought he might be, where he was from, who his parents were, and where he worked. The only question she could answer was where he worked. She felt so ashamed because she didn't know the man she was married to.

After leaving the hospital, she lived with her sister Marie for six months. It took her four years to get herself together and, in 1963, she divorced her husband. She found a job and devoted her life to raising her son Barry, pouring all her affection, love, and care on him. She was determined to be a good mother and protect him. Barry was a good student, an outgoing boy with strong moral values who was liked by everyone.

When he was 14, some neighborhood boys approached him to join a group that sold drugs, but he refused. This refusal cost him his life. They held him down and injected a lethal shot into his arm. He was found in the basement of an abandoned building.

This brutal attack and murder proved to be the final breaking point for Cynthia. She was on the verge of a nervous breakdown. She couldn't control her grief. She wanted to die. After Barry's death, she stood at the window calling for him for many months. Finally one of her neighbors, Miss Meyers, who had lost three children in violent deaths on the streets, sat with her to let her know that she understood her grief, but showed her that she had to go on with life.

One night after this conversation, Cynthia had a dream in which she saw two roads converging. One was leading to the dark, the other was going toward the light. She was told that she could choose which way she wanted to go. She chose the light, and slowly but surely she started to want to live again. This was the turning point and the beginning of her self-improvement journey.

Determined to raise herself up, she borrowed books from the library and took reading and writing classes at Rev. Ike's church in New York. She learned about positive thinking and applied it. At first, she was embarrassed to let others in the reading classes know she couldn't read, but she kept going until she learned.

As she got better and gained more confidence, she enrolled in courses at Toro College, taking psychology and computer classes to understand herself and obtain some job skills. She took out a student loan to pay for the classes. Her interest in fashion design led her to courses at Mayer's School of Fashion Design, from which she received a certificate. She started a home business making clothes.

Through intensive therapy, Cynthia learned how to

express herself and uncover the real Cynthia that was buried underneath the physical and emotional scars. At age 58, she felt that she was just starting to "come out" and learn about her "true unlimited potential." Still, something was missing. That "something" was a high school diploma. She worked hard for two years and fulfilled her dream at the age of 60.

Her mission is to share her life experience so others might come to know they aren't alone in their abuse, that they can identify and overcome abusive relationships through prayer, meditation, and counseling.

KEY STRATEGIES FOR BRAVERY AND RESILIENCE

Bravery comes through experience. Developing resilience results from your personal journey. People do not all react the same way in stressful situations. What might work for one person may not work for another. Practice these ideas and see which ones work best for you.

- Avoid seeing crises as insurmountable problems.
- Realize that change is a part of living. Accepting circumstances that can't be changed can help you focus on circumstances that you *can* alter.
- Take a positive view of yourself by developing confidence in your ability to solve problems.
- Take care of yourself by paying attention to your own needs and feelings. Do activities that you enjoy and find relaxing. It helps keep your mind and body primed to deal with stressful situations.
- Although you can't change the fact that stressful events happen, you can change how you respond to these events. Look beyond the present to a better future.

Chapter 5

I Will Survive:
Never Give Up

"Nothing in the world can take the place of persistence. Talent will not: nothing is more common than unsuccessful men with talent. Genius will not: unrewarded genius is almost a proverb. Education alone will not: the world is full of educated derelicts. Persistence and determination alone are omnipotent."
—Calvin Coolidge

How do you "never give up"? This really isn't a skill to hone, but rather a mindset. Persistence beats resistance. The more you're tempted to call it quits, the more you need your never-give-up mindset.

Most cases of never giving up fall into two categories. The first category involves reaching the goals you've committed to. When you build a house, you build it to handle rough weather. When you make a commitment, you must prepare for rough times and be willing to weather the storms. Have you ever heard of someone getting married "for better or worse; let's try it for 90 days"? Of course not. A strong initial commitment will make a never-give-up mindset easier.

"Patience and perseverance have a magical effect before which difficulties disappear and obstacles vanish." —John Quincy Adams

The other category involves circumstantial situations, or things that happen to you while you're "living your life." You have no control over these things, but you must deal with them. Later in this chapter, you'll read about my divorce, which is a good example of a circumstantial situation.

"By perseverance, the tortoise won the race!" —Anonymous

Never-Give-Up Mindset

In Illinois many years ago, a young man who had only six months of schooling ran for an office in the legislature. Of course, he was defeated at the polls. He started his own business, but when it failed, it took him 17 years to pay off the debts incurred by his deadbeat partner. He fell in love with and became engaged to a charming lady, but she died and he had a nervous breakdown. Then he lost a race for Congress and failed at trying to be appointed to the U.S. land office. He wanted to become a candidate for vice-president, but didn't get that opportunity. Two years later, he lost a Senate race. He ran for office one more time and was elected president of the United States. His name was Abraham Lincoln.

Another hero is Christopher Reeve who starred in the Superman movies. In 1995, he broke his neck when he was thrown from a horse. Left completely paralyzed, he lived for more than nine years after the accident. Reeve had a great attitude about life and actively spoke out for issues he believed in.

This chapter is filled with similar stories. Remember, not giving up is a *mindset* rather than a *skill* that can be taught. I believe the best way to adopt this mindset is to surround yourself with committed people. If you don't know anyone personally, become familiar with the stories of people like Lincoln and Reeve—and the women in this book.

This chapter has been written to remind you about persistence—this important element of success—so you can focus on it in your life. The quote at the beginning of the chapter says it all. Now it's up to you to add or strengthen the elements of persistence and determination to whatever you're doing in life.

Draw on your power of persistence and never, ever, ever give up. There will be times when you will want to just quit and say, "This is enough; I can't go on," or "I want to stay stuck because it's more comfortable." You might begin to feel hopeless and ask yourself, "Is it really worthwhile?" The answer is yes! Whatever discomfort you feel is only temporary; it, too, shall pass.

THE NIGHTMARE OF MY DIVORCE

During the time of my divorce, I thought that my feelings of hopelessness and sadness would never end. I know the power of determination and persistence carried me through those hard, hard months. Believe me, many times I felt discouraged and wanted to give up. Twenty-five years later, I'm glad I used that innate power of persistence that you also have inside of you.

With my divorce, my biggest nightmare occurred right before my eyes and I never saw it coming. My self-esteem, which was fragile and bare, crumbled. My heart was shattered, my very being was shaken, and I was devastated. My perfect, intact, nuclear family was shredding thread by thread and I could do nothing about it. My children were losing a father whom I desperately wanted for them. And I was being left alone.

Even though it happened 25 years ago, I still remember the Sunday morning when my husband called me into the family room and told me he wanted a divorce. A divorce! I couldn't believe it. He wanted to destroy our family. How could he? What kind of bastard was he? I knew the fabric of our marriage had been unraveling, but I never imagined he wanted to leave.

Every emotion tumbled over me—the biggest being fear, failure, and doubt. I pleaded to go for marriage counseling. I begged him to reconsider. All I could see was that I was going to be left alone to raise three children with no father, just as my mother was left to raise four children on her own. I could only see loneliness, fatherless children, and broken dreams.

My own fragile self-esteem cracked and I found myself begging for my life, begging not to be left alone, begging for my dreams, begging for my sanity, begging to continue to accept the crumbs he might offer. To no avail. I humiliated myself further by promising to lose more weight. You see, I was fat and foolishly thought that was the reason he was leaving. After all, his lover was thin.

All my pleading and begging did no good. He was determined to leave. He refused to admit it was because of the affair he'd been having with my so-called friend. Rather, he said he wasn't in love with me anymore. He said he was moving out to live on his own.

It actually happened one Sunday—on a beautiful, sunny morning. I remember my pain seeing him pack his clothes and leave. I couldn't bear it, so I went for a walk and cried all the way to the beach. After all these years, I can still recall the intensity of that morning. It was the end...of what? Of a dream? Truthfully, it marked the end of having a husband who hadn't worked for two years, refusing to take a job to support his family. Since I was supporting the family anyway, what was it the end of, really?

In retrospect, my divorce marked the beginning of a journey of survival, self-growth, self-sufficiency—and ultimately happiness. I couldn't see that outcome at the time. After all, I had just been mortified, humiliated, and jilted by a man who didn't love me, and I couldn't do anything about it. I had been ready to settle for crumbs from a man I thought I'd spend the rest of my life with—a man who was unavailable to me, who had several affairs over the course of our 12-year marriage, who disappeared for days and didn't tell me where he was, who pretended he wanted the same things I wanted. Why did I want such a man in my life? Why was I willing to settle?

After my return from the beach that Sunday morning, he was gone and I was left to care for the children, ages ten, five, and three. My oldest daughter understood what was happening, but the other two didn't. They remember little of what occurred. He promised to support them, but I should have known that the same irresponsibility he showed *during* the marriage would continue.

At first, he made a few attempts to see the children, but he gradually stopped. Although he lived in the same state, less than an hour away, he put several months and often years in between visits. Still, I allowed him to see the children whenever he wanted despite the fact that he didn't support them. The only real money I got was when his salary was garnished for a short-lived job. Another time, the judge threw him in prison and wouldn't allow him out until he paid me $1,000. Someone he knew came up with the money by the end of the day. Unfortunately, that was the last support we got from him for the next 20 years.

I had two choices. I could either allow myself to drown, or force myself to swim. I decided to swim upstream. Dusting off the sorrow and wiping away my tears, I got to work. This was the biggest turning point in my life. I prayed and continued attending the weight support group I'd been a member of for two years. At my job, I was making $18,000 a year—not enough to support three children, take care of a house, and handle all the other things that come with survival.

For example, during the first year without my husband, I had to replace the roof and the septic tank. Many times, I had no oil to heat the house. I considered selling the house but quickly squashed that idea; I wanted stability for my children. I was concerned that after their father walked out, uprooting them would be too traumatic. So I got a summer job teaching macramé in adult education centers to make ends meet. In the meantime, I discovered every consignment store and tag sale in the area to clothe my children.

I will never forget the friend who gave us her daughter's clothes, mailing them to me after she moved. Nor will I forget the friend who put oil in our heating tank one winter, or the friend who paid my car insurance so I could drive to work, or the friend who lent me her car until I could afford to buy one. (My ex-husband took our brand new car and didn't make payments. Because the loan was in my name, I had to pay that loan.)

My husband's family never offered a hand, nor did I ask for help. I didn't ask my family members for help either; they had their own problems and struggles. So I suffered in silence. I figured out what I needed to do and did it. I became handy around the house, making a lot of mistakes along the way. I painted, did plumbing, carpentry, cut the grass, and similar tasks. In retrospect, I don't know how I did it. I only know that I intended to survive. Gloria Gainer's song "I Will Survive" became my theme and my anchor. It assured me that indeed I would survive.

I worried how I would find a new partner who would

want to be with me and three children. Well, it happened. I did find someone who cared for me because I was indeed special. He liked my independence and determination.

Before long, I decided to go back to school because, in the education field, more degrees equal more money. I also knew I liked variety and didn't want to be an elementary teacher forever. So I found a babysitter for the children and attended graduate school for a degree in counseling, then later earned a doctorate in administration from Columbia University.

In the meantime, my daughters grew up beautifully. My dreams for them came true when they all graduated from college. Today, at the ages of 36, 32, and 29, they have developed into independent women.

I have come a long, long way from those murky days after my divorce. This story of struggle, fortitude, courage, and determination is meant to inspire you—to empower you to never, ever give up. You, too, have the same inner strength and courage to survive any obstacles.

WILMA'S STORY:
FROM PARALYSIS TO WORLD-RENOWNED ATHLETE

Wilma Rudolph, the 20th of 22 children, was born prematurely and her survival was doubtful. At four years old, she contracted double pneumonia and scarlet fever, leaving her with a paralyzed leg. At age nine, she removed the metal leg brace she had been dependent on, she was so determined to walk without it. By 13, she'd developed a rhythmic walk, which doctors declared a miracle.

That same year, she decided to become a runner. She entered a race and came in last. In fact, for the next few years, she came in last at every race she entered. Everyone told her to quit, but she kept on running. One day she actually won a race. Then another. From then on, she won every race she entered. Eventually, this little girl, who was told she would never walk again, went on to win three Olympic gold medals!

NAKATO'S STORY: THE SINGING MOTHER

The crowd clapped and cheered as the curtains opened at the prestigious nightclub. The open curtains revealed three talented jazz singers—including Nakato, a backup soprano for Grammy Award winner Denise Williams.

That night, Nakato felt "on top of her game"; she had attained her lifelong dream as a professional jazz singer.

No one thought this African American—a teenage mom on welfare for many years—would ever arrive at this glorious moment. It took 20 years of hard work and determination for her to be in the spotlight on this stage.

When Nakato was 13 years of age, she found out she was pregnant—a situation filled with shock and denial. Worried about her parents' reaction, she didn't break the news to them until her 14th birthday when she was three months along. They reacted to the news with disappointment and anger. Their daughter—one of ten children—had so much promise. The baby's father, seven years her senior, offered to marry her, but her parents turned him away, saying Nakato was too young.

Getting an education was the highest priority in her family. After the baby was born, her parents fully expected Nakato to finish school, but they left her on her own to figure out how to cope with a baby and school at the same time. She couldn't rely on them for babysitting; she had to take her baby wherever she went. Thankfully, she received welfare money from the state to pay for daycare and some of her expenses.

Believing that "she had made her bed and she had to lie in it," her parents demanded she complete school or she couldn't live in their house. So they enrolled her in a program for young mothers in which she completed eighth grade and prepared for high school.

Though the reality of having a child so young was sober-ing, Nakato made the same mistake again and got pregnant by a popular boy at school. Because she refused to consider abor-tion or adoption, she braced herself to tell her parents…again. At 16, she gave birth to a second daughter. This time she had company; two of her sisters were also pregnant.

Their parents had a hard time accepting and forgiving all three of their daughters, especially Nakato. The turmoil created within the family almost led to their parents' divorce. They stuck by their daughters by providing a physical place to live, but offered no emotional support. They made it clear these children would be their daughters' responsibilities, not theirs.

With four babies and seven siblings plus their parents in the house, it was bursting at the seams. Although she received some emotional support from her sisters, Nakato still had to fend for herself and two babies while attending high school. At times, she felt trapped in a sea of hopelessness. She had to share her room with her daughters, who were awake at all hours. Many nights, she couldn't sleep and went to school feeling groggy.

Nakato dug deep within to find the strength to juggle all of their schedules—bringing her daughters to daycare on the bus, doing schoolwork, and maintaining a part-time job. She had to struggle to finish high school, struggle to hold down her $4.00/hour job, and struggle to create a stable life for her family.

Coping with the pressures overwhelmed Nakato. Her parents, too, felt overburdened; they had already raised ten children and suddenly had four more to feed. While a teenager, Nakato thought their emotional indifference made them mean and hateful, not helpful. Later, she realized they were forcing her to face her own responsibilities.

During these years, Nakato numbed her feelings to forget how painful her life was and focused on survival. She had no time for self-pity or any other thoughts about herself. Instead of going to the movies or hanging out with friends like most teens do, she could only focus on two things: caring for her babies and getting her education.

All this time, Nakato never lost faith in the future. She was determined to prove she could make it on her own. Through hard work and diligence, she graduated with her class.

Many low-paying jobs followed high school graduation, and Nakato quickly realized she couldn't make it financially unless she went to college. So she applied and was accepted into a small liberal arts college where she majored in music theatre and physiology. Her first love was music, but her teachers told her she would never make it as a singer. She started believing their words and felt discouraged.

Because she enjoyed fitness and dance, her major in physiology suited her well. These studies prepared her to become a paid fitness trainer, work that helped support her through college. She completed her program in three years by taking 20 credits a semester while she worked two jobs. She accomplished this with the help of her brother who took care of her children while she pursued her goals. After graduation, she became the first African American to work at the exclusive Golden Door Spa in California. Then she started her own private fitness practice while working for a fitness center, training and mentoring young trainers.

All the while, Nakato never abandoned her first dream and passion of singing. In the background, she heard a little voice telling her, "Yes, you can sing." Deep down, she knew her jazz soprano voice was waiting to blossom and be appreciated.

Through the years, she continued taking voice lessons

until she found her "niche" in jazz singing. She started performing in small nightclubs with a trio of musicians, performing many gigs in the San Diego area.

Then the day finally arrived. Nakato learned that Denise Williams needed two backup singers for her performance at Kimball's East. She practiced, auditioned for the spot, and got it. She would finally take her place on stage with a Grammy Award winner. All her hard work paid off as she made her dream of singing professionally a reality. Clearly, Nakato believed in herself and in her ability to stay focused, disciplined, and patient. She never gave up.

MARTHA'S STORY: OVERCOMING PREJUDICE

Martha, the only child of a working-class domestic, believed she was the chosen one. In 1950, she became the first African-American operator to be hired by the Southern New England Telephone Company in the state of Connecticut. Her hometown of Norwalk is a small suburban town not far from New York City. African Americans made up a small percentage of Norwalk's mostly white population. At the time, membership in civic organizations, church groups, and clubs, as well as participation in community activities, were all segregated, with one exception—going to the movies.

When Martha got the call to work at the New England Telephone Company in her hometown, she felt excited and surprised. In fact, a whole year had passed since she had applied, so she had given up on ever being hired. She had even started her own secretarial business. It didn't provide steady work, so the possibility of a steady job was timely and appealing. She jumped at the opportunity.

From all the times she had gone to that office to pay her telephone bill, Martha knew that no other African-American operator worked there. Still, she was confident in her abilities and believed the color of her skin wouldn't be an issue. As one of only a few African Americans in elementary and secondary school, she'd become used to being among white people. She expected to be accepted for who she was—a capable and hardworking person.

Martha reported to work on a bright sunny day in the spring of 1950. She was greeted on the sidewalk by a senior operator assigned to be her trainer. "What a nice thing for her to do," Martha thought, feeling encouraged. During her training, the vice president of the company came down from New Haven, Connecticut, to observe how she handled the customers. Later, she learned this had never happened before.

Smiling her contagious smile, Martha said "hello" and "good morning" to her co-workers every day as she passed through the office, but no one responded to her cheerfulness. No friendly greeting echoed in the halls. No welcome smiles came from the operators. There were no introductions at all, just blank stares.

"What am I walking into?" she wondered. Still, she told herself, no matter what, she would prove she could do anything she set her mind to. She'd be willing to pay the price for the independence this job gave her to support herself and her daughter. She vowed to become the best telephone operator in Norwalk.

As the weeks and months wore on, still no one talked to her or even acknowledged her presence, as if she were invisible. Martha continued to be surrounded by this conspiracy of silence—a silence broken only by the voices of customers on the telephone.

As a result of this abuse at work, tension and stress built up inside her. But Martha said nothing. Instead of having "two cheeks" like the first black professional baseball player Jackie Robinson did, she developed "four cheeks" to deal with the silence. But she refused to allow her colleagues to see how painful and isolated she felt, saving her pent-up emotion for home where she could freely let off steam. Her friends often saw her act moody and disagreeable as the tension carried over into her personal life.

The abuse continued. One time, the union was hosting a party and every union member who wanted to attend had to sign up. Because the party was scheduled on her birthday, Martha thought it would be a good birthday celebration.

Alas, signing up for the party became a big deal. Three times, she added her name to the list and three times it got erased, even when she wrote it in pen and placed tape over her name. Then someone actually removed the tape to blot out her name.

When she brought this to the attention of the union representative, the leader clearly stated that this show of prejudice would not be tolerated. However, Martha decided if her fellow union members were going to act so mean toward her, she didn't need to be associated with them. How could she feel comfortable at the party if her co-workers went to such lengths to stop her from attending?

The raw hostility that pervaded her workspace made Martha realize that any other black person hired into an all-white environment would likely be treated the same way. Her individual solution called for using her mind to focus on her responsibilities and "make the grade," regardless of how isolated she felt.

On the job, Martha had no time for boredom because the phones rang constantly. She wasted no time on self-pity, knowing her co-workers could control the environment but not her thinking. She adopted an indifferent attitude and acted as though she didn't give a damn. She especially didn't want them to know what havoc the silence played in her head and on her emotions.

To further cope, Martha evoked her strong spiritual beliefs in God who had delivered others from similar situations. This spiritual approach helped her pray for those who were silently persecuting her.

Over time, the phone company hired more African-American operators. Little by little, some of the white operators broke the silence toward the black women and began communicating with her, too. Martha continued to work. Her diligence and persistence eventually paid off because, as the years went by, she received many promotions. When she retired after 35 years, she had earned the title of Business Representative. In that position, she supervised the setup of phone services for corporations in the area.

Martha's thirst for using her powerful mind continued into retirement when she was able to enroll in the Norwalk Community College. There, she earned a degree in criminal justice.

Martha's focus on her goals—and her courage and determination to stick with them despite abusive treatment—finally brought its rewards. She accomplished her first goal of purchasing a home in 1959 and achieved her second one by sending her daughter Diane to college. Martha was especially proud when Diane became a teacher and, later, an elementary school principal.

KEY STRATEGIES FOR NEVER GIVING UP

Behaving with persistence is a conscious decision; you *can* become a persistent person. Napoleon Hill gives eight factors that persistence is based upon:

1. Definite purpose—knowing what you want
2. Desire—achieving what you truly desire
3. Self-reliance—having the belief to carry out your plan
4. Definite plans—writing an organized plan
5. Accurate knowledge—knowing that your plan is sound

6. Cooperation—being with others who will help you develop persistence
7. Willpower—concentrating your thoughts on obtaining your goals
8. Habit—developing persistence as a habit

Consider doing these practices regularly:

- Write down your definite goal and back it up with a strong desire to obtain it. (For example: I will set aside $1000 every month so I can put my children through college.)
- Have a plan of action. How are you going to make it happen? What do you need to do? (For example: I will meet with a financial planner to discuss my monthly budget.)
- Close your mind to negativity and discouraging influences. Self-talk can be the most damaging. Watch what you are saying to yourself. (For example: I will observe my thoughts and make sure they agree with my goal. I will not listen to any opinions that are not in alignment with my goal.)
- Surround yourself with a group of people who will encourage you but also hold you accountable to follow through on your actions. (For example: I will have a phone call with my mentor once a week to discuss my progress.)
- The words Winston Churchill gave in a speech on Oct. 29th, 1941, are still applicable today. He said, "Never give in—never, never, never, never, in nothing great or small, large or petty, never give in except to convictions of honor and good sense. Never yield to force; never yield to the apparently overwhelming might of the enemy."

- Believe in yourself. Believe in your goals. Stay focused. Never change your goal—just your plan. Replace the plan if necessary, but not your goal.

Persistence must become a way of life if you want to succeed. By learning to overcome problems and barriers, you can become a tremendous person. What do you do when you are tempted to give up and quit? Here are three keys to build up your level of persistence! Ann Rusnam www.getresults-quicker.com)

Key 1: Overcome Your Obstacles

What's standing in your way? Is it something you can control? Is it something you can change? Sometimes things we can't change or control are actually not roadblocks, but tools in our hands—we just haven't seen them that way.

Key 2: Keep Your Eyes on the Goal

Always keep your desired accomplishments in front of you. For example, a Christian's goal might be to behave like Christ in every area of life and not let worldly temptations lead him or her away from that goal. Keep your eyes on your goal.

Key 3: Take the Next Step

You're in a race—the race of your life. Run it one step at a time, even when things are difficult. Don't let difficulties set you back. Take each day as it comes, and take each step as you can.

Chapter 6

I Am More than Enough: Cultivate Your Strengths

"Most Americans do not know what their strengths are. When you ask them, they look at you with a blank stare, or they respond in terms of subject knowledge, which is the wrong answer." —Peter Drucker

Because you have been born with a combination of innate, God-given talents unique to you, your strengths come from cultivating and focusing on your talents.

I especially like the analogy used by Edward "Chip" Anderson and Donald O. Clifton in their book, *Soar With Your Strengths.* They compare talents to "diamonds in the rough" and strengths to "diamonds that show brilliance after they have been carefully cut and polished; just as finished diamonds start as diamonds in the rough, strengths start as talents. And just as rough diamonds are naturally found in the earth, talents are naturally found within you. But while diamonds are refined with blades and polishing wheels, strengths are produced when talents are refined with knowledge and skills."

You, too, have the opportunity to polish your diamonds and become successful. When you study people who have excellence in their lives, you can see how the process unfolds. First, they become aware of their talents, then they refine their innate skills through education and training. They gain experience and finally develop their skills into strengths that bring them abundance, joy, and a place in the "flow."

Oprah Winfrey is an excellent example of a woman who strengthened her innate talent of talk and her zest for reading. She used every opportunity to share her diamonds in church, contests, and college, where she majored in English. These settings gave her the opportunity to gain insights and experience. Today, she's developed her strengths into a multi-million dollar empire. (See www.oprah.com for more about Oprah's empire.)

Jackie's Story: Turning Wounds into Service

Jackie had been a happy, trusting, country girl who remembers the days when the family was so poor, they didn't have toilets in the house. She remembers using leaves and newspaper for toilet paper and receiving food baskets from the Salvation Army at Thanksgiving and Christmas.

Jackie's mother, known as the biscuit lady, baked biscuits every Sunday. She sent Jackie, the fifth of six children, to deliver biscuits to an elderly minister, Rev. Jones. One day a few years ago, Jackie ran into Rev. Jones, who reminded her of the "fun" they used to have when she was a little girl. She looked at him in disgust as horrible memories flooded her mind—memories of repeated molestation, violation, and abuse at an early age for three years. She remembered the fondling and the touching. She remembered feeling being dirty and unworthy, feeling ashamed, feeling helpless— sensing that something must be wrong with her and this was not right. She was too naïve, innocent, and trusting at eight years old to understand what was happening.

Afraid of being blamed or not believed if she told anyone, Jackie went completely inside herself. She felt alone with no one to protect or rescue her. "My God," she recalled, "I was only eight years old. His thanks and appreciation for the biscuits was to molest me every Sunday for three years." The abuse only stopped after Rev. Jones got assigned to a Pentecostal church in another part of the state.

Jackie was always a good student, but during this time, her grades went from A's and B's to an F in Mr. Askbro's fifth grade class. "His is the only teacher's name I remember from elementary school," she recalled. "He never bothered to find out the reason for the drastic change." Identified as a discipline problem, she was repeatedly suspended from school for fighting and even got arrested for it. "I was so angry with life! I hated the world and trusted no one," she explained.

Jackie's mother was a cold and uncaring person. She, too, made no attempt to find out the reason for the sudden change in her daughter's school performance and behavior. Her mother only focused on survival, which meant cleaning houses to provide a home and food for the family. She didn't know how to create the warm and nurturing environment her children needed to thrive. In addition, education wasn't important to her or to Jackie's father, who couldn't read or write. At work all the time, he wasn't available to spend time with her or her siblings. So left on her own to pass or fail at school, Jackie didn't complete her high school education.

At age nine, Jackie learned that she couldn't even trust her older sisters who made fun of her after she got her first menstrual period in school while wearing a yellow skirt. Jackie didn't have a clue what was happening. "I thought I'd been cut and tried to stop the bleeding with band-aids," she recalled. "How could I confide in such sisters who didn't offer support when I most needed it? How could they make fun of my embarrassment?"

When Jackie was 12, she was again sexually abused, this time at the hands of her mother's 21-year-old brother. Her mother had sent Jackie to baby-sit her uncle's child in the afternoons until he came home from work. Her uncle had seen Jackie take a 17-year-old boy up to her room and threatened to tell her mother about it if she didn't cooperate. Effectively he blackmailed her into having sex with him. She was terrified of being found out so she allowed herself to be abused. This abuse occurred repeatedly until she was 15. Again, she told no one.

Early on, Jackie had lost her faith in God, since her first abuser was a "man of God" and the second was a family member. "If I couldn't trust a minister or a family member, whom could I trust?" she thought.

At the end of junior high, her counselor encouraged Jackie to enroll in a technical high school to study home economics and learn to be a domestic because, he told her, "You're not college material." Instead, she chose to attend the comprehensive high school.

The turning point came for Jackie when she was 15. A kind guidance counselor in tenth grade believed that this minority student had the power to change the negative direction of her life. She called Jackie into her office and told her she had two choices: She could continue to get poor grades, drop out of school, and become a teenage mother, or she could turn things around. She recommended an "upward bound" program called Trio at the University of Bridgeport. This program helped students like Jackie believe in themselves and pursue a college education. It provided study skills, workshops in self-esteem, speakers who shared their humble beginnings, preparation for the SAT exams, and help completing the college application and scholarship process.

"I didn't want to be like my sisters who had all become teenage mothers, or like my brothers who were all incarcerated. I decided to give it a try." Jackie took advantage of all the workshops and courses offered. She said, "They showed me another way."

In the company of students who were also poor and

wanted to better their lives, Jackie became exposed to new opportunities. She lived on the college campus during the summer and went on tours of other colleges, where she talked to students who shared their experiences and inspired her to pursue a college education. The inspirational speakers who came to the campus showed her that she could achieve and rise above her circumstances. "They inspired me to be a somebody, not a statistic."

After graduation from high school, Jackie received a full scholarship to a small women's liberal arts college in Massachusetts. Her parents told her to "get a job" after graduation because, they said, college wasn't important or necessary. However, with encouragement from her teachers and counselors in the Trio program, she entered the predominately white all-girl private Catholic college with dreams of becoming a social worker.

She studied sociology because she wanted to help other children who grew up as she had. Her Spanish teacher and a local candy store owner always praised her knack for speaking Spanish words like a native, so she majored in Spanish, which she speaks fluently today.

In this college town, Jackie found herself in an extremely racist community, as she said, "Because the manager of the local department store feared I would shoplift, the nuns told me I wasn't allowed to go there. I was the only black person in the town."

All through college, neither her parents nor siblings encouraged her. They remained aloof, never visiting her in college. In fact, Jackie's sisters were often jealous of her achievements and they taunted her, saying, "You think you're better than us, you college girl."

However, as the years rolled by, Jackie locked away the memories of her abuse deep in the recesses of her mind by focusing on her studies, still never telling anyone.

After graduation from college, Jackie went to work for the state's Department of Children and decided to specialize in child sexual abuse. During the many specialized workshops and intensive trainings she took, Jackie came face to face with the memories of abuse she'd locked away for years. Working with children who had gone through similar experiences brought her old painful memories to the surface. A skilled interviewer, she was able to not only understand their fears but got them to share their "secrets." By helping these children and using the strategies she'd learned in her training, she began to heal herself.

Jackie came to understand that her own abuse wasn't her fault, that she was an okay person. She also learned that, as the victim, she wasn't at fault. This healing freed her spirit and allowed her to pursue her lifelong dream of earning her MSW degree.

As the memories of her childhood pain became more intense, Jackie sought comfort in a church. This started a deep relationship with God and the formation of a strong spiritual belief. "I thank God for my healing from the inside out. It's God grace that healed me, restored my sense of self, and ordained me to use my negative experiences for His glory."

TURNING TALENTS INTO STRENGTH

When is the last time someone asked you to identify your strengths? You likely never hear that question or think about it either. On the other hand, how often do people criticize you or tell you about your weaknesses? How much do you think about them yourself? The truth is, most people focus on their weaknesses a lot more than their strengths.

Everyone has natural talents; some people have a few and others have many. The key to success is to hone your talents and turn them into strengths. But before you do that, you must find out what your talents are—if you don't already know. Don't worry if that takes some investigation; our society doesn't put a lot of emphasis on people discovering their talents.

When you refine your talents to the point at which you can provide consistent, near-perfect performance in certain activities, you have several *strengths*. And when you develop your these strengths even more, you move closer to fulfilling your natural potential as an individual.

The strengths you focus on should be things you enjoy. If you're good at something that you don't particularly care to do or are bored with, find something else to focus on, or find a more rewarding way to use that strength.

Often, people assume they have to work really hard to be good at their strengths. Sometimes, they aren't aware of their strengths because their natural abilities come easily to them. For example, in the movie "Good Will Hunting," the lead character's mathematical ability surpassed that of the greatest mathematicians in the world, but it was so easy for him that he considered it "no big deal" and, in fact, it bored him.

Successful people focus on their strengths rather than their weaknesses. In fact, by focusing on strengths, you diminish your weaknesses. Consider Oprah Winfrey or Celine Dion. They discovered their talents, developed those into strengths, and organized their lives to apply their strengths and enjoy success. You are no different than these celebrities are.

To discover what your talents are, try different activities and pay attention to which ones come naturally. Especially notice the ones you enjoy immensely and feel willing to do what it takes to develop them. Choose ones in which you lose track of time because you're so absorbed in them. For example, a friend of mine recently discovered she has the gift of feeling people's energy—a strength she could use to learn

Reiki and help others as well as herself.

As you try different activities, you'll find new talents and interests. Not only will this help you discover potential strengths, but it will probably give you a fresh outlook on life. During this discovery process, keep in mind that every person has his or her own definition of success and achievement.

What talents can you develop into strengths? Do you have a beautiful singing voice, the ability to run extremely fast, the gift of being a good communicator or organizer? Do you have a knack for gardening or cooking, understanding a foreign language, having a soothing or healing touch? The list could go on and on.

> "The real tragedy of life is not that each of us doesn't have enough strengths, it's that we fail to use the ones we have. Benjamin Franklin called wasted strengths 'sundials in the shade.'" —Unknown

TAKING A STAND

One of my ambitions was to become an administrator at the high school where I lived. I'd completed my credentials: 15 years of teaching and five years as a guidance counselor, plus earning a doctorate degree from Columbia University. I was ready!

When the opportunity arose, I applied for the position. I felt confident the interview went well and knew I was highly qualified for it. Two weeks later, I heard from other sources (not the superintendent who interviewed me) that I didn't get the job. Imagine my disappointment when I heard who had landed the job—a white male whose credentials were far inferior to mine.

I felt betrayed by the superintendent who, five years earlier, had assured me that in a few years, they would need people with my energy and creativity for administrative positions. In fact, he's the one who encouraged me to seek my administrative degree.

Previously, I had applied for several positions at the elementary level and was told that my lack of administrative experience precluded me from getting those positions. I accepted that because the people who got those positions had more experience, but in this case, the position of the assistant principal at the high school level didn't require previous experience. I felt that I was being denied an opportunity for which I was more qualified than the person they gave it to.

Thinking deeply about the injustice, unfairness, and obvious difference in credentials between me and the other applicant, I couldn't help but wonder if my race and gender were factors. I decided to find out about my legal rights.

I consulted an attorney who specialized in discrimination. After I told him all the details, he assured me that he had never seen such blatant discrimination. I knew I had to take a stand and file a lawsuit against the board of education and the superintendent. Needless to say, I was scared and frightened. I had never done anything like that before.

My attorney wrote to the superintendent, informing him of our intention to pursue the matter further if the injustice wasn't corrected. The letter stated, "From everything I am able to discern in the course of my investigation of this matter, Dr. Barnett is a victim of racial and gender discrimination, and the action of the Board of Education is in clear violation of both federal and state discrimination laws."

After four weeks and several consultations with my attorney and the superintendent, I was offered a position as assistant principal at a middle school. I refused it, because it wasn't the position I had applied for. A few days later, I received a call telling me to report to work at the high school to which I had applied. I was elated that I had won the fight, but I knew there was more agony to come. After all, by going into a school where I wasn't wanted, I was walking into a hornet's nest. The principal didn't want me there, nor did the other assistants, and the secretaries considered me a militant. In fact, it was worse than I imagined. I felt like some of the leaders in the civil rights days who had to break down walls to get justice, yet this was 1992. I remember praying, "God, you walk in front of me and I will walk behind you."

The principal started by giving me my assignments and that was it—no explanations, no showing me around the school, no nothing! I didn't expect a warm welcome, but I was shocked at this ice-cold reception. The only people who welcomed me were the custodians. They even assured me of their support because they felt proud I had fought for the position. I was also blessed with a great secretary who became my friend and right-hand person. Her support and encouragement kept me going in those early days.

I soon realized that the principal had set me up for failure by assigning me two-thirds of all the responsibilities, a heavier load than the other two experienced assistants carried. I looked at it analytically, then broke down the many duties into bite-sized pieces.

During this time, I prayed a lot and began my serious spiritual journey, concentrating on my personal growth. I knew I needed to be strong to survive in this negative atmosphere. I read Dale Carnegie's book *How to Win Friends and Influence People*, then took the Carnegie course. Practicing these strategies on the principal who didn't want me, I was determined to earn his respect the Dale Carnegie way. He was my evaluator and I did not want him to give me a negative evaluation, plus I didn't intend to fail. In Malcolm X's words, I succeeded "by any means necessary." Not only did I practice Dale Carnegie's strategies, I also initiated and elicited my principal's evaluation every month, then followed up with a written summary of each meeting and what I planned to do with his suggestions for improvement. After initiating these monthly meetings for three years, I never got a negative evaluation from him. In fact, I believe he came to respect my work.

By continually working on my personal growth over the next ten years I was there, I became a woman who had gained great strength and confidence; I felt I could do anything. When people asked me how I survived that time in my life, I said, "With a strong spiritual foundation and putting God in the driver's seat, a person can do anything." Now that I've retired from the school system in my new "refired life," I intend to inspire other women. I assure them that, no matter what obstacles they face, they too have the inborn strength to overcome, survive, and fulfill their dreams. With the help of God, they can do, have, and be anything they want.

KEY STRATEGIES TO DEVELOP YOUR STRENGTHS

1. Make a list of the specific talents (no more than three) that come easily for you. You may not see them as "special," but if you're naturally adept at them, write them on your list.
2. Determine your commitment to dedicating money and time to developing your talents.
3. If you're willing to do what is needed to develop these strengths, set some deadlines. Research classes, activities, or counselors who can help you expand your talents.
4. Find a mentor or someone else who will support you in your efforts to excel.
5. Put a measurable return on your investment. Create a list of reasonable accomplishments you hope to attain after developing your talents.
6. Think big! Who's your role model; who's an expert in your field? Study these people and their development

strategies. Adopt any of their strategies that you like, putting them to work for you.

One of the best books I've read about strengths is *Now, Discover Your Strengths* by Marcus Buckingham and Donald O. Clifton, based on a Gallup study of more than two million people. After purchasing the book, you can take an online assessment to help you determine your five top strengths. Once you've identified your dominant natural talents and assessed the extent you've developed them into strengths, ask yourself:

- What do I want to achieve?
- What is my purpose?
- What are my goals?
- Which are my most important natural talents that I want to develop further?
- Which of my natural talents can contribute most to achieving my purpose and goals?
- What do I have to do to develop these talents into strengths?
- What knowledge do I need to learn to develop these talents?
- What weaknesses do I need to manage to develop these talents?
- What skills do I need to acquire or improve to develop these talents?

The key to developing your strengths is to remain persistent. Many people benefit from working with experts. If you believe you need more than the help of a mentor, by all means, hire a coach or consultant.

The end result—peace and confidence in your personal and professional life—will be well worth the cost!

Chapter 7

Newly Found Power: Let Go of the Past

"Forgiveness is the experience of peacefulness in the present moment. Forgiveness does not change the past, but it changes the present."
—Dr. Fred Luskin

Several years ago, while en route from a speaking engagement, I stopped in the airport gift shop and purchased *Tuesdays with Morrie: An Old Man, a Young Man, and Life's Greatest Lesson* by Mitch Albom. I read the book from cover to cover during the flight home. I found Morrie's story so potent and meaningful, it touched a chord in my soul. Mostly, it reminded me how short life really is. In fact, reading that book moved me to call my ex-husband, with whom I hadn't communicated for years. I told him three simple words: "I forgive you." I gave no explanation and there was no need for one; he knew about the abandonment I was referring to.

Those three words changed my life. Suddenly, my grudges, bitterness, and resentment that had held me prisoner evaporated. Being "baptized" in this way, I experienced a divine peace within. I'd kept the hurt alive too long, allowing it to rent free space in my head. Instead, I started to look at the good in the past relationship rather than focus on the abandonment. I saw him anew as a human being, not as a "heel." I felt more compassionate toward him, despite his wrongdoing. And I began to fully appreciate my three beautiful daughters and considered myself lucky to have them in my life. I felt a great sense of freedom.

"A wise man will make haste to forgive, because he knows the true value of time, and till not suffer it to pass away in unnecessary pain."
—Samuel Johnson

You might be wondering, "What does forgiveness have to do with freedom?" The answer? Everything.

Forgiveness is your gift at the end of the healing process. Forgiving someone isn't for that person; it's for *you*. Have you ever imagined, in your wildest dreams, that from injustice could come a gift that didn't require erasing, changing, or forgetting what happened? It's true.

Have you ever heard that you can't get to second base with your foot on first? This applies to life. You simply can't move toward your future when you're hanging onto your past.

A NEW UNDERSTANDING

This chapter is intended to empower you with a new understanding of forgiveness and give you a step-by-step strategy to accomplish it.

First, open your mind to let in new ideas about forgiveness. If you're not in a place of forgiveness in your life right now, put your current ideas aside and let this information help you. If you're already doing well with forgiveness, you'll enjoy this chapter immensely.

Let's look at what forgiveness is *not*. Many people confuse forgiveness with condoning behavior, letting someone off the hook, even forgetting the incidents or pretending nothing happened. Others think it means giving up or admitting defeat. Still others think that condemning or telling offenders about their wrongdoing is forgiveness when it's actually dishing out moral superiority. True forgiveness is none of these things.

Rather, it happens internally, moving you toward your future. By allowing you to put aside emotional baggage, you lighten your load—and actually feel lighter. Forgiveness allows you to stop letting someone continue to hurt you. It turns destructive thoughts into quieter, healthier thoughts. It can help you interact better with others. It even helps you feel at peace with yourself and with God.

For example, if a car pulls out in front of you in traffic, your initial reaction might be to get angry at the driver. But practicing forgiveness could help you swiftly deal with your anger. Immediately using words of forgiveness lets you refocus on the thoughts you had before the incident—which is far more important than giving energy to that bad driver you don't even know.

If forgiveness is that simple, then why do people hold grudges? Why don't they forgive easily? Why do they hang onto their grudges while trying to lead normal lives? Because *not* forgiving has its benefits.

Not forgiving gives you an excuse for whatever is wrong with you and your life, which in turn could actually bring sympathy. You might think, "If only that hadn't happened…"

Not forgiving protects you from being harmed again in the same way. You keep up your guard, believing it reduces the risk of rejection, deception, abuse, betrayal, or other emotional hurts.

Not forgiving breeds the "good person" illusion. If there are "good" and "bad" people, and whoever did something to you was "bad," then obviously you are "good." However, once you practice forgiveness consistently, you no longer define your world in black and white. You have to deal with shades of gray, and that can feel scary.

What do people want in their lives? I'm sure you'll agree

that most people want less anger, fear, and stress in their life, as well as more optimism and better health. What about increased energy, inner peace, and openness to receive? These are just some of the benefits of practicing forgiveness. It's all about you and your life—not other people and their lives.

When you harbor resentments, you focus on them rather than yourself. I say, you deserve more of your energy and attention than they do, right? Absolutely! If a friend called and said, "Let's get together and discuss ideas about improving our emotional health," would you say, "I can't, I'm too busy focusing on grudges and resentments right now"? Yet until people go through the forgiveness process, that's exactly what they're doing.

Because forgiving and not forgiving both have benefits, why should you choose forgiveness? Here's why. It gives you a feeling of wellness and freedom, as well as showing you positive self-esteem. It's empowering to realize that you no longer need to hold your grudges, resentments, hatred, or self-pity. It means you no longer allow the "guilty" parties to live rent-free in your head. Besides, these negative feelings and emotions can be better used in a positive way to move your life forward.

When you understand forgiveness, you see new possibilities for yourself.

"Good nature and good sense must ever join. To err is human, to forgive is divine." —Alexander Pope

LIKE A POTTER MOLDING CLAY

You might be asking, "How do I forgive?"

Forgiving doesn't happen instantly. It's a process, so take baby steps at first. Think of a potter slowly molding, shaping, and reworking clay to make a pot. In a similar way, you might start by refraining from saying bad things about those who've offended you. If you pray, you could make a habit of praying for them in a broader context, not as those who hurt you.

For example, my friend was molested as a child by her uncle when he was in his late teens. She learned that her uncle was once a sad, depressed little boy who suffered from abuse. Knowing this helped her think of him as a real person who also had a childhood. Going forward, she felt compassion, while at the same time she didn't condone his actions.

There is no time limit on how long going through a forgiveness process should take. Don't compare yourself with others, for the deeper the hurt, the more time the process will require. Be prepared. The work can sometimes be painful. In a construction zone, roads get torn up before they're rebuilt, but the finished product is much better than before construction started. So it is with the process of forgiveness.

ABA GAYLE'S STORY: FORGIVING A MURDERER

Aba Gayle's journey toward forgiveness started in 1988, but her story really begins in 1980. After her daughter Catherine was stabbed to death at the age of 19, Aba Gayle lived in a cloud of deep dark rage for eight years. She revealed this rage to no one. With a mother fragile from open-heart surgery, two children in medical school, and a husband who refused to talk about Catherine—nor having any belief in God or religion—Aba Gayle survived by being calm and not causing waves.

When Douglas Mickey was sentenced to death in 1982 for Catherine's death, Aba Gayle believed that when this horrible villain was executed, she'd be healed of her pain and all would be well again. Not knowing any other way to think, she developed a passionate lust for revenge, which she cultivated over many years.

Six years later, Aba Gayle took a course in meditation

and, for the first time, began to realize far more exists in this universe than she could pick up with her senses. She wanted to know more, so she located a beautiful Unity Church in Auburn, California. In that environment, she was like a sponge—soaking up information, listening to the teachings, and studying books on different philosophies, religions, and enlightened beings. Ultimately, Aba Gayle learned that she is a beloved child of God and that all people are one with the universe—on earth to love each other without exception. She came to an understanding within herself that God is a loving God and that the only hell is the one created in the human mind.

Aba Gayle devoted the next four years to meditation and spiritual studies. During that time, she saw a video introducing A Course in Miracles and got her first glimpse of the healing power of forgiveness. The video showed a man who survived the Holocaust and was able to forgive not only the German people but also the actual guards who had killed every member of his family. Something about his story clicked for Aba Gayle. For the first time, she began to believe she could forgive the man who killed Catherine.

After moving to Santa Rosa, she began attending a study group for A Course in Miracles as well as classes to study *The Science of the Mind* by Ernest Holmes. Her group spent a lot of time discussing forgiveness. After many hours of study, prayer, and discussions, she thought that perhaps she could forgive Catherine's killer and relieve herself of frustration and suffering. One night, a classmate suggested that she let the murderer know of her intent. That idea outraged her! She felt out of sorts as she drove home, but during that drive, she distinctly heard a voice that said, "You must forgive him and you must let him know!"

The voice was so clear and persuasive that Aba Gayle didn't sleep at all that night. Here is an excerpt from the letter that she typed at 4:00 a.m.:

"…I was very angry with you and wanted to see you punished to the limit of the law. You had done irreparable damage to my family and my dreams for the future.

After eight long years of grief and anger, I started my journey of life. I met wonderful teachers and slowly began to learn about my God-self. In the midst of a class studying A Course in Miracles, I was surprised to find that I could forgive you. This does not mean that I think you are innocent or that you are blameless for what happened. What I learned is this: You are a divine child of God. You carry the Christ conscious-ness within you. You are surrounded by God's love even as you sit in your cell. There is no devil; there is only the good-ness of God. The Christ in me sends blessings to the Christ in you.

Do not look to me to be a political or social advocate in your behalf. The law of the land will determine your fate. Do not waste your last days on earth with remorse and fear. Death as we know it is really a new beginning. Hell does not exist except in our conscious minds.

I hope that this letter will help you to face your future. There is only love and good in the world regardless of how things may appear to you now. I am willing to write to you or visit you if you wish.

I send blessings to you and to your children…"

Just sending the letter gave Aba Gayle the most incredi-ble feeling of joy, love, and peace. She knew the instant the mailbox clicked shut that she didn't need anyone to be executed for her to be healed. At that point, it didn't matter if she received a response from him. She felt healed by that simple act of forgiveness.

Douglas did write back with words of gratitude. Aba Gayle was totally amazed at the kindness and gentleness of the writer. He expressed remorse and sorrow for the crime, stating that he fully understood how empty such words might sound. She could tell from reading his letter that he was intelligent and well read. He had clearly spent years studying for answers himself. He wrote, "The Christ in me most gratefully accepts and returns blessings of divine wisdom, love and charity to the Christ in you."

He also wrote, "…I would gladly give my life this instant if it would in any way change that terrible night…"

Douglas took Aba Gayle up on her offer to visit him. More than 90 days later, she found herself in a visiting room for death row inmates. She looked around with surprise as she realized she didn't see a single monster in that room. Rather, it was filled with ordinary men. More than that, everywhere she looked, she saw the face of God.

Then she met her daughter's killer and the two of them talked for over three hours. They talked about his mother and her death. They cried together. They talked about Catherine. As they discussed their losses, Aba Gayle realized that the night Catherine lost her life Douglas Mickey lost his future.

After that visit, Aba Gayle began to spend time visiting men on death row. During this time of her mini prison ministry, reporters sometimes ask her if any of the men on death row have committed crimes that are too awful for her to still treat them with compassion. She responded, "I don't deal with their crime. I don't deal with that part of them. I deal with the God spirit within him or her. That is the truth of their being. It is the truth for every one of us."

If someone had told Aba Gayle in 1980 that Douglas Mickey was a human being and not some kind of horrible monster, she would have been terribly insulted and outraged. Today, Aba Gayle works hard to demonstrate that killing is not necessary and that violence begets more violence. (I invite you to visit her website and read more about her work at www.catherineblountfdn.org)

"He that cannot forgive others breaks the bridge over which he must pass himself, for every man has need to be forgiven."
—Lord Herbert

KEY STRATEGIES FOR LETTING GO OF THE PAST

When you hold resentment toward someone or some condition of the past or present, you are bound to that person or condition by an emotional link that's stronger than steel. This blocks your prosperity and keeps you tied to the very person or condition you want to get free of. Practicing forgiveness is the only way to dissolve that unhappy link and free yourself to a better, more productive life.

Forgiveness Heals, Forgiveness Prospers—Exercise 1

Make a list of everyone you have held resentments toward.

_____

_____

_____

_____

_____

_____

_____

_____

I suggest you read your list every night and morning. Pick two or three people, put each name in the blank below, and say the last paragraph. You may want to include yourself for forgiveness, too.

"_____, I fully and freely forgive you. I let you go. You fully and freely forgive me. All things are cleared up between us now and forever. There is no condemnation in you, for you, or around you. You are now free."

(Permission to reprint this exercise is granted by Vicki@excellentcoach.com)

Letting Go of the Past—Exercise 2

I did the following process after I had forgiven my ex-husband and have shared it with many coaching clients and participants in my workshops.

First, choose a person in your life whom you know well and have a grudge against. On a piece of blank paper, draw a heart in the center of the page and write down what that person did to you. Then fill the rest of the page with blank hearts. In each, write a word or phrase that describes something about the person for which you feel grateful. Write down something he or she said to you or did for you. Also write something important about the relationship: small things, big things, current things, historical things.

After you have filled in each of the hearts, hold the page at arms' length and notice how the grudge gets lost in the sea of gratitude.

As you think about this activity, reflect on these questions: Are you able to see the person in a different light now? Have your feelings for the other person changed? Are there positive parts of the relationship that you now remember? Do you notice any changes in your mood and how you feel about yourself?

I firmly believe that if you decide you're not going to let the past control your future, you can learn to break down the walls of hurt and pain that hinder you from forgiving others and living fulfilled lives. Holding on to pain and hatred causes anger and bitterness. In turn, anger and bitterness cause stress and anxiety. These emotions can cause a variety of other health problems.

I know it's possible to embrace happiness, experience joy, and have success. The choice is truly up to you!

Chapter 8

Count Your Blessings: Cultivate an Attitude of Gratitude

"There are two ways to live your life. One is as though nothing is a miracle. The other is as though everything is a miracle." —Dr. Albert Einstein

What does the word gratitude mean to you? If you have to give it a lot of thought, then you could practice more gratitude in your life. Gratitude is an appreciative awareness for something received, whether it's tangible or intangible.

"If the only prayer you say in your entire life is 'thank you,' that would suffice." —Meister Eckhart

My friend wants her four-year-old daughter to be in the habit of practicing gratitude, so every night when she puts her to bed, she asks her daughter what she's thankful for. Sometimes her daughter points to the lights, the windows, the roof. Other times, she mentions people, things, or even nice weather. There is no right or wrong answer; the point is to get in the habit of being thankful and happy about what she has.

Oprah Winfrey suggests writing down what you are grateful for every night before going to sleep. She maintains that if you focus on what you don't have, you'll never have enough, but if you focus on what you do have, it expands in your life.

"As we express our gratitude, we must never forget that the highest appreciation is not to utter words, but to live by them." —John Fitzgerald Kennedy

Practicing gratitude has many benefits: It builds confidence and self-esteem; it keeps you feeling positive; it's always available; it wards off jealousy; and it's free! Do you know people who don't own much, but their lives seem rich and happy because they appreciate what they have? You probably also know people who own all kinds of "things" but are never happy. The bottom line is gratitude is a choice. Having "enough" isn't measured by what you possess; it's determined by how you choose to perceive what you do have.

Give the gift of gratitude to yourself. Notice that I didn't say, "Buy the gift of gratitude for yourself." Not only is gratitude free, but the riches that an attitude of gratitude can bring you can't be bought. When you do this, you'll be surprised at how your life will transform, personally and professionally. You'll become like a magnet that will attract what you want for yourself.

It's impossible to be thankful for something you don't feel you deserve, so if you start showing sincere thanks, good things will come your way. You'll finally feel that you deserve them.

A SINGLE MOM AND A MERCEDES

A perfect example of this is a woman named Shellie, a single mother of five children with two of them still living at home.

Shellie needed a vehicle. A friend told her about a Mercedes that was for sale for only $2,000, although it was worth much more. Shellie was able to buy that car, but it didn't occur to her until weeks later that she never would have had this opportunity if she hadn't called the seller. Even though someone kindly put the information into her hands, she actually made the phone call. A year or two before, she never would have called because she simply thought she didn't deserve such a fine car. A Mercedes was definitely out of her league. When she realized she invited that opportunity into her life because she'd changed her thinking and her attitude, she was amazed at the power of something so simple and so available.

SIMPLE, BUT NOT EASY

Practicing gratitude is simple, but not easy. Perhaps you don't make time for it or focus on what you don't have. Perhaps you're a perfectionist (which make it almost impossible to be grateful). But just like you can't be wet and dry at the same time, *it's impossible to focus on what you don't have and practice gratitude at the same time.*

If you study successful people, you'll see that they constantly express an attitude of gratitude. Certainly, developing that attitude became a big part of their success. Have you heard that whatever you give will come back ten-fold? This is also true of gratitude; it's a gift to yourself and everyone around you.

A simple, effective way to practice gratitude is to make giving thanks part of your everyday life. Sarah Ban Breathnach, author of *Simple Abundance*, speaks about the importance of keeping a Gratitude Journal. At the end of each day, she encourages readers to record five things that they feel grateful for in their Gratitude Journal. I purchase her Gratitude Journal at the end of every year and have been keeping it for the seven years in a row. What a blessing it has been! It has helped me remember and give thanks for the simplest things—like being grateful I can open my eyes in the morning and take a breath. Writing in it helps me focus on the little things that make each day special, like walking into my beautiful home, savoring the gorgeous flowers, and enjoying the warm smiles and giggles of my grandchildren.

ITZHAK PERLMAN'S STORY: A MAN OF TALENT AND GRATEFULNESS

As a child, the famous violinist Itzhak Perlman had been stricken with polio. He wore braces on both legs and walked with crutches, so getting on stage for his concerts was no small feat.

As soon as he appeared for a special concert in New York one night, the audience applauded, then respectfully waited as he slowly made his way across the stage. He took his seat, signaled to the conductor, and began to play his violin. No sooner had he played the first few bars than one of the strings on his violin snapped! At that point, Perlman was close enough to the beginning of the piece that it would have been reasonable to bring the concert to a halt while he replaced the string. But that's not what he did. He paused a moment, then signaled the conductor to pick up just where the orchestra had left off.

Perlman now had only three strings with which to play his solo. He was able to find some of the missing notes on adjoining strings, but where that wasn't possible, he had to rearrange the music on the spot so the melodies held together.

Audience members could see how he spontaneously rearranged the symphony through to the end while still playing with passion and artistry. When he finally rested his bow, they sat for a moment in stunned silence. Then they rose to their feet and cheered wildly. They knew they just witnessed an extraordinary display of human skill and ingenuity.

Perlman raised his bow to signal for quiet. "You know," he said to the audience, "sometimes it's the artist's task to find out how much beautiful music you can still make with what you have left."

We have to wonder, was he speaking about his violin strings or his crippled body? And is this true only for artists? Do we all lack something? Are we challenged to answer the question: Do we have the attitude of making something of beauty out of what we do have, incomplete as it may be? (The Path of the Soul Dr. Allan Morris)

If you've lost your job, but you still have your family and health, you have something to be grateful for. If you can't move around except in a wheelchair, but your mind is as sharp as ever, you have something to be grateful for. If you've broken a string on your violin and you still have three more, you have something to be grateful for.

OVEREATING LEADS TO GRATITUDE

My cultivation of an attitude of gratitude started 30 years ago when I first became grateful for being a compulsive overeater. That might sound strange and cause you to wonder how I could possibly be grateful for being a compulsive overeater. Here's the reason.

When my youngest daughter was six weeks old 30 years ago, I was obese. I was told by my former husband that I had a small face and a big body. At that time, I never looked beyond my face because I felt so ashamed of my body. My weight had spread from 120 pounds to more than 200 pounds on my five-foot two-inch frame. I used having three children as an excuse, plus I had tried every diet in the world—pills and more. I thought my husband was divorcing me because I was fat. The stark reality was that I couldn't stop eating.

"If you haven't got all the things you want, be grateful for the things you don't have that you don't want." —Anonymous

"When we focus on abundance, our life feels abundant. When we focus on lack, our life feels lacking. It is purely a matter of focus." —Susan Jeffers

Finally, when I walked into a 12 step program to deal with my obesity, I knew I belonged there. Of course I came in to lose weight, but I found more than ideas for living without food. Through this program, I received the true joy of life, the gift of cultivating the attitude of gratitude. I discovered that it was not about the fat on my body, but about the way I thought about myself. The program itself wasn't about food, but about how to live the best life possible by looking at my life—physically, mentally, and spiritually.

Being overweight is no longer an issue for me. I have maintained a normal weight for the past 25 years. Yes, I still struggle with not being able to eat like "normal" people do, but what's really important? For me, it's more important to continue to live the way I was meant to live, to live at my best, and to continue to cultivate that attitude of gratitude. The program I've been following has taught me discipline and showed me how to deal with other areas of my life. Like the rippling circles created from throwing a pebble in the water, the program set in motion those circles of life that now protect me and show me how to live completely.

I'm so grateful for being a part of this program that saved me from the hell (and probably early death) of obesity.

It wasn't easy to cultivate an attitude of gratitude as I went through my trials and tribulations raising three daughters on a small salary. And without any financial help from their father, I didn't feel grateful for the longest time. In fact,

I wondered what I did to deserve such a life of hardship.

In retrospect, taking this 12-step program proved to be the training ground for me to become a creative problem solver, and for this I am truly grateful. As I cultivated this attitude of gratitude, I not only began to see its benefits, but I felt drawn into the magic of giving thanks on a regular basis. That's true every day of my life.

Can you understand why I sing the song of gratitude daily?

Gift of Gratitude

Gratitude comes in all colors, all sizes and shapes. Wouldn't you agree that the most grateful people are little kids? When they fall down and get up while learning to walk, they smile. When they accomplish something and openly show their appreciation for living, they laugh. It's fun to see how they acknowledge gratitude in the little things. I believe the more people show appreciation for the little things, the more they really appreciate the *big* things when they show up.

If you ever have trouble with feeling grateful, turn to the David Pelzer story which starts with the book *A Child Called 'It'*. In this horrific story of the abuse Pelzer suffered as a child, he describes days he was grateful for warm temperatures outside. That meant he'd be able to stay alive on those days instead of nearly freezing to death on his cot in the garage with no blanket. It's amazing how stories like his can put small complaints into perspective.

You have this free gift called gratitude inside of you; all you have to do is use it. Just saying a simple "thank you" is enough.

"Beginning to tune into even the minutest feelings of...gratitude softens us...if we begin to acknowledge these moments and cherish them...then no matter how fleeting and tiny this good heart may seem, it will gradually, at its own speed, expand." —Puma Chodron

"Feeling gratitude and not expressing it is like wrapping a present and not giving it."
—William Arthur Ward

KEY STRATEGIES TO CULTIVATE AN ATTITUDE OF GRATITUDE

1. Take a ten-minute thank-you walk.

When you feel thankful, it's physiologically impossible to be stressed. By being thankful, you activate the part of your brain associated with positive emotions and deactivate the part that ignites fear and stress. Walking is a powerful mental and physical energizer. When you walk, you produce endorphins and flood your brain with "happy" transmitters that make you feel joyful and energized. Taking a thank-you walk helps you decrease the stress that zaps your energy while triggering the release of hormones and neurotransmitters that boost your energy.

Schedule your ten-minute thank-you walk in the morning or afternoon. Write down what you are thankful for: your family, kids, garden, the fact that you have a job, health, your ability to see, walk, hear, and so on. If figuring out how far to go to walk ten minutes causes anxiety, simply set a timer or alarm for five minutes, walk until it goes off, then turn around and go back.

2. Take a daily gratitude walk.

As you walk, look around in nature and express gratitude for the trees, the ocean, the birds etc. Focus on being thankful and let this feeling elevate your step and your mood.

"Let's be grateful for those who give us happiness; they are the charming gardeners who make our souls bloom." —Marcel Prouse

3. Write a letter of thanks.

This strategy helps you experience the wonderful feeling you get from acknowledging the people you appreciate. So many times, you can easily forget to tell others you notice their efforts. Write a letter or poem to someone in your life whom you would like to acknowledge. Instead of mailing it, sit down with that person and read your letter or poem to him or her. Notice that person's reaction—and your own feelings—as you read it. Trust me, doing this is *life changing*. I tried it with my life mate and it moved him to tears.

4. Every day, find an opportunity to express your gratitude.

The expression can be as simple as saying a sincere "thank you" to someone who holds the door open for you, or it can be as elaborate as the gratitude letter described above. Just make it a habit to build gratitude into your daily life.

5. Fill up a gratitude box.

Get a box (about the size of a shoebox) and have your children help you decorate it. On a piece of paper, ask them to write down one thing they are grateful for every day. Put the papers in the box. At the end of the week, read what they wrote at one of your family meals. If you don't have children, do this exercise with your partner or housemate, or just do it for yourself.

Chapter 9

We are the World: Making a Difference

"It is one of the most beautiful compensations of this life that no man can sincerely try to help another without helping himself." —Ralph Waldo Emerson

Sooner or later, most people ponder the question, "Why am I here?" The people who seem to be the happiest and live the most rewarding lives are those able to give back to society, those who leave a legacy.

If you want happiness for an hour, take a nap.
If you want happiness for a day, go fishing.
If you want happiness for a week, take a vacation.
If you want happiness for a month, get married.
If you want happiness for a year, inherit a fortune.
If you want happiness for a lifetime, help others.
—Chinese Proverb

If this concept is completely beyond you, chances are you're so wrapped up in the financial rat race that you can't see your way out right now. Don't worry; it will come. When you practice gratitude and all the other suggestions in this book, your future will start to take shape. Remember, if you keep doing what you're doing, your life will likely be the same five years from now. In reality, you've got nothing to lose by applying the principles taught in this book. Maybe leaving a legacy lies completely beyond your realm of possibility. But don't look too far ahead; take baby steps toward change and a positive future.

When my last daughter left for college, I began to feel sad, empty, lonely, and unfulfilled. I started singing the blues. What was I going to do with my time and energy besides doing my work? One night, I had a vision and heard a certain "call" to use my experiences as an educator. The "call" appealed to my concern about the growing academic and digital divide between minority and white students. I was led to create a program that would provide enrichment courses in reading, writing, and technology on Saturday mornings. I named the program Saturday Academy. Each student would pay $50 for eight weeks of academics. With just this idea and no money to back it up, I presented it to leaders of one of our local churches. They gave me space and recruited children from their Sunday school classes. I decided to volunteer my time.

So many children signed up for this Saturday Academy that I had to hire six teachers. Because of it, my name was submitted to CBS television, who sent people to videotape the students and interview me. I was honored for this work (along with 14 other recipients) at a luncheon. What an awesome experience. And the gift for me? I gratefully received a lot more than I gave.

Lezlie's Story: Riding Program for Kids

This story, reported in *Sports Illustrated*, Fall 2004, highlights a horse trainer named Lezlie Hiner who had a fervent mission to help African-American children avoid violence and despair on the streets of Philadelphia. She involved them in a most unusual sport, polo—a game mostly played by the wealthy. Hiner organized a polo squad made up of inner-city kids and trained them to take part in the interscholastic national championships. She gave them the opportunity not only to learn to ride and care for horses, but also to play polo, the sport of kings.

With a small grant and a fierce determination, Hiner started the riding program in exchange for working at the stables. As the kids improved their riding, she started them on playing polo. The rest is history. They became so good that they ended up competing in many tournaments.

About the game of polo, she said, "There is a lot of snobbery, but what I'm finding, more and more, is that when the kids get out on the field and play, they command a lot of respect," says Hiner. "They're good. That's what breaks down the barriers."

"Ask not what your country can do for you; ask what you can do for your country."
—John F. Kennedy

Giving back to society benefits not just a few, but all of us. It can be as simple as offering to deliver meals to the elderly and mentoring a troubled student, or as substantial as running for elected office in your local school district, your city, your country. Whether you focus on your neighborhood, your community, or the world, giving back to society is important. I encourage you to participate in your own way. The gift will be yours.

KEY STRATEGIES FOR MAKING A DIFFERENCE

Look at the months of the year that have themes dedicated to different causes, including Women's History month, Breast Cancer month, Heart month, and so on.

- Select a theme that is dearest to your heart.
- Send a donation to a sponsoring organization.
- Seek out the activities for that month and take part in them.
- Walk or run to raise funds for a particular event featured that month.
- Create your own funding event to raise awareness for the cause.
- If you can't find a cause to support, start one that resonates with you and organize an event around it to raise awareness.

For example, children's organizations are always looking for volunteers and donations. Therefore, consider donating your time to the 4-H program, which touches the lives of thousands of young people by helping them reach their potential and building leaders of tomorrow. To get involved, look up your local cooperative extension office in the phonebook or contact your county 4-H extension agent. Offer to get involved in the most successful youth educational and service organization in the world. That's all you have to do, no matter what time of year, where you're from, or how much you previously know about 4H. (To find a website for your state's 4H group, go to www.4HUSA.org)

Volunteering as a mentor is another great way to give back. Mentoring is a powerful method of developing inclusion. It increases self-esteem, which also leads to increased student achievement. Mentors not only work individually with students, but also in classrooms with teachers. Call a nearby school today and volunteer to be a mentor.

Chapter 10

Be Good to Yourself: Focus on You

"This time, like all times, is a very good one, if we but know what to do with it."
—Ralph Waldo Emerson

I am so excited for your future! There has never been a better time than right now to take charge and call the shots in your life. The information is already in your head; you must put it into action. You get rid of your fear of taking action by *taking action*. After all, how can you be afraid of doing something that you're in the middle of doing? Above all, love yourself and choose activities that nurture that love. (If you're looking for a popular resource to help, check out the Extreme Self-Care Program on my website at www.peakperformancesolutions.com)

In previous chapters, I've shared stories of people who have struggled and bounced back from overwhelming obstacles. When a woman puts herself first and truly frees herself to serve her higher purpose, she can be ten times more loving and giving and helpful than when she is appeasing others. An important part of this transformation is "living in the now."

"Present-moment living, getting in touch with your 'now,' is at the heart of effective living. When you think about it, there really is no other moment you can live. Now is all there is, and the future is just another

present moment to live when it arrives. One thing is
certain, you cannot live it until it does appear."
—Dr. Wayne Dyer

Have you ever stopped and categorized your thoughts?
If you did, you'd probably find that most thoughts relate to
something that *has* happened or something that will happen.
That means you constantly dwell on the past or the future,
even in the subtlest of ways. Sure, you might be planning
your day or enjoying the sweet memory of an evening out
the night before. But how often do you sit back and take note
of the grand moment you're currently in? If you're like most
people, not often enough.

To explore this subject further, pick up the wonderful
book by Eckhart Tolle called *The Power of Now*. He says that
if you realize you are not present, then you become present.

"So don't worry about tomorrow. Tomorrow will
worry about itself. Each day has enough trouble of its
own." —Matthew 6:34, The Holy Bible

SHARPEN YOUR SKILLS

Make sure you sharpen your skills on a daily basis—what
management teacher Dr. Stephen Covey calls "sharpening
the saw." The length of time doesn't really matter; what
matters is the consistency of being aware of the importance
of focusing on *you*. That way, savoring every moment by
"living in the now" helps you increase your prosperity and
daily happiness.

Deciding to "stop singing the blues" requires action. It
requires change. If you still struggle every time you need to
make a decision, think about this: *When your fear of things
staying the same is greater than your fear of change, you'll take*

action toward your goal. How uncomfortable is it for you to stay the same? Remember, you're a beautiful, courageous soul. Your ability to reach your dreams is within your grasp.

I recommend that you read this book several times to fully grasp its meaning. The exercises at the end of each chapter put action behind reaching for your dreams and goals. Each time you reread this book and do the exercises, you'll gain something fresh from doing so. You'll be motivated and inspired in different ways to live your dream.

One of the ladies who worked on this book went to my web site and took the Quality of Life Test before she read the book. Then she took the test again after reading it. The first time, she looked at her low score and, that day, made a decision that she wanted to improve her future. She took action. The second time she took the test, her score was twice as high as the first time. I don't share these results to brag about my influence, but to inspire you to continue your personal work so you can affect someone's life the same way I did. There is no greater satisfaction!

You have an obligation to this planet to do something useful with the gift you have received—your life. Your obligation is simply to create your own happiness. One book of higher learning suggests that in the afterlife, people will be held accountable for those pleasures in life that they didn't take advantage of.

Yes, pleasures are important. You don't live to exist, to take up space, to take energy away from others. So stop singing the blues. Give joy to yourself: grow, love, explore, help, learn, inspire, motivate, lead, and celebrate!

KEY STRATEGIES FOR FOCUSING ON YOU

Make self-care a priority in your life. When you begin putting yourself first, you will have more energy, feel better about yourself, and enjoy better health. Taking care of yourself is so personal that I would like to share an assessment that I found to be valuable and helpful. It was developed by Beth Dargis and is used here with her permission. (For more information, go to www.encouragingcoach.com)

HOW GOOD ARE YOU AT TAKING CARE OF YOURSELF?

Yes___ No___ 1. Do you take time for yourself every day?

Yes___ No___ 2. Do you exercise 5 times a week for at least 30 minutes?

Yes___ No___ 3. Do you get 7-8 hours of sleep every night?

Yes___ No___ 4. Do you brush and floss your teeth twice a day?

Yes___ No___ 5. Do you have a haircut you love?

Yes___ No___ 6. Do your nails look great?

Yes___ No___ 7. Do you get together with a friend at least once a month?

Yes___ No___ 8. Do you have a hobby you do at least twice a month?

Yes___ No___ 9. Do you have a spiritual discipline like prayer, meditation, or church?

Yes___ No___ 10. Do you watch less than one hour of TV a day?

Yes___ No___ 11. Do you say no to requests that aren't right for you?

Yes___ No___ 12. Do you usually know how you are feeling?

Yes___ No___ 13. Do you usually know what you need?

Yes___ No___ 14. Is your home organized enough to make you feel peaceful?

Yes___ No___ 15. Does your environment support your goals?

Yes___ No___ 16. Do you have something fun to look forward to every evening?

Yes___ No___ 17. Do you take frequent breaks during the day to recharge?

Yes___ No___ 18. Do you have a nurturing daily routine?
Yes___ No___ 19. Do you have a relaxing bedtime ritual?
Yes___ No___ 20. Do you know what you are passionate about?

Now add up all your "Yes" answers.

17-20   I am very proud of you. You are taking excellent care of yourself. Now you can delve further into things like getting massages, simplifying your life, and getting rid of as many stressors as you can.

13-16   You know how to take care of yourself. Now do it consistently.

9-12   You may value yourself, but seem to put yourself last too often. Set an evening aside just for you every week with no outside obligations. Cull your calendar to get rid of unimportant meetings, etc. Turn off the TV after an hour. Put in a daily half hour for you in your appointment book. Let go of unrealistic standards of how much you can get done in a day. Cut your "to do" list for the day in half. Now use that time to work on one thing on the checklist above until you form a habit. Then move onto another one.

4-8   You feel guilty every time you take time for yourself. You need to realize that your family, friends and work don't want an empty vessel. They want a vibrant, authentic, energetic you. Talk with your family about how you want to start taking better care of yourself. Discuss how they can help out more. If they are supportive, see if they are open to having you be accountable to them. Which thing from the above checklist do you think would have the most impact on your energy and well-being? Work on that action until it becomes a habit.

0-3   You don't really think you deserve to take care of
            yourself. You feel unimportant in the scheme of
            things. Kids, family and everyone else always
            come before you. Journal your feelings about self-
            care. Write down ways you give to others. Notice
            that you are needed. The world wouldn't be the
            same without you. Write down your best qualities
            and skills. Often we think we don't have any, but
            if you ask someone else they will say that they've
            always admired you for... We think if something
            comes easy to us, then it can't be a real skill. When
            in reality, the stuff that comes easy is what we do
            best and are meant to do. You are just as important
            as the other people in your life. Shine for them!
            Pick an easy, non-threatening action to start
            caring for yourself. Maybe you can drink one more
            glass of water or take 5 minutes alone. Start small
            and work your way up.

            I urge you to take action now. Apply the princi-
            ples in this book every day to have more "music"
            in your life. As you do, I am confident that your
            actions will put a skip in your step and you will
            live the life of your dreams with joy, satisfaction,
            and harmony.

An Invitation from Dr. Cynthia

In the near future, I will be compiling a file of stories of all the women who have been inspired by this book. Feel free to email me at <u>Doctorcynthia@stopsingingtheblues.com</u> Your story just could appear in my next book. You are also invited to sign up for my online newsletter "The Self-Empowerment Booster" at www.peakperformance-solutions.com